SHIPWRECK DIVING

By Daniel Berg

A COMPLETE DIVER'S HANDBOOK
TO
MASTERING THE SKILLS OF WRECK DIVING

Foreword by Steve Bielenda

DISCLAIMER

Please be aware that the information contained in this book is only a supplement to proper wreck diving instruction. Reading this book does not qualify a diver to do penetration dives or to participate in any activity beyond the capabilities of his own qualifications.

Please use the information contained within this book as a basic guideline, and let good diving skills, common sense, and courtesy lead you and your dive buddy to safely enjoy exploring these underwater time capsules.

Library of Congress Catalog Card No. 91-071029
ISBN: 0-9616167-5-X

FOR ADDITIONAL COPIES, WRITE TO:
AQUA EXPLORERS, INC.
P.O. Box 116
East Rockaway, N.Y. 11518
Phone/Fax (516) 868-2658

FOREWORD

Shipwreck Diving is a complete guide to mastering the skills and enjoying the sport of recreational wreck diving. This 88 page softcover book is packed with information and expertly illustrated with over 80 color photographs. Dan Berg, a long time friend and dive partner, describes all of the basics including equipment modifications, and how to navigate on a wreck and be able to return to the anchor line after the dive. Dan also details wreck penetration and underwater communication techniques as well as how to locate artifacts and preserve them. Dan covers diverse topics such as underwater mapping, shipwreck research, treasure hunting, photography and how to catch lobsters. This exciting new book titled *Shipwreck Diving* tells all the tricks of the trade that until now have only been learned through years of experience. Shipwreck divers of all caliber will find information on how to make their dives safer, and more enjoyable.

This book should be read by all who have or are planning to explore shipwrecks. Experienced wreck divers and the neophyte alike will find *Shipwreck Diving* informative rewarding and entertaining.

Captain Steve Bielenda, President
Eastern Dive Boat Association.
Owner/Operator R.V. Wahoo

"Steve Bielenda is a salty professional scuba diver, teacher and salvager who's risen to the top of his underwater trade". Nick Karas, NEWSDAY. Photo by Daniel Berg.

ACKNOWLEDGEMENTS

I would like to thank the following for their time, knowledge and information: First of all, my wife Denise for the hours she spent editing and proof reading; Captain Steve Bielenda, who gave freely from his time earned wreck diving knowledge and Jozef Koppelman, who spent countless hours not only in the water with his cameras, but also in the writing of the photography section. Janet Bieser, Bill Campbell, Mike DeCamp, Bill deMarigny, Carl Fismer, Hank Garvin, Gary Gentile, Charlie Guttilla, Jon Hulburt, Rick Jaszyn, Hank Keatts, Dennis Kessler, Robert Lewis Knecht, Stephen Lombardo, Mike McMeekin, Ed Tiedemann, Jeanne Tiedemann, Edna & Teddy Tucker, Keith Wipprecht. Also my diving partners, Bill Campbell, Steve Jonassen and Rick Schwarz, Dive Rite Manufacturing, Beuchat, Wenoka Sea Style, DUI Dry Suits Fisher Metal Detectors, and Garrett Metal Detectors. I am also grateful to my father Winfred Berg for his continued support, my Brother Donald Berg and Aaron Hirsh for their technical advice, and my sister-in-law Christine Berg, who spent many hours editing. Without the assistance and dedication of all listed, this text would not have been possible.

UNDERWATER PHOTOGRAPHY

I would like to acknowledge and sincerely thank the following for their beautiful underwater photographs. A picture is worth a thousand words, and the photos taken by these professionals truly capture all the beauty, mystery, thrill and excitement of wreck diving. I am grateful to Jozef Koppelman, who spent countless hours photographing and reviewing photographs for use in this book as well as Steve Bielenda, Mike Burke, Bill Campbell, Steve Frink, Carl Fismer, Jon Hulburt, Robert Lewis Knecht, Rick Schwarz, Jeanne Tiedemann, and Keith Wipprecht.

HOW TO USE

All topics covered within this text are listed in the index. One can read this book cover to cover or just pick certain topics to enhance ones own wreck diving knowledge. I'm sure divers of all caliber will find something of interest, whether it be the basics of finding their way back to the anchor line or preservation methods for those priceless artifacts.

ABOUT THE AUTHOR

Photo by Steve Jonassen.

Dan Berg is a P.A.D.I. (Professional Association of Diving Instructors) Master Scuba Diver Trainer. He is a Specialty Instructor in Wreck Diving, Night Diving, Search and Recovery, Underwater Hunting, Deep Diving, Dry Suit Diving, U/W Metal Detector Hunting, U/W Archeology, and has written and teaches his own nationally approved Distinctive Specialty courses in Shipwreck Research, Shipwreck Sketching and U/W Cinematography. Dan also holds certifications in Rescue and Environmental Marine Ecology. He is on the board of advisors and is an instructor for C.U.R.E. (Center for Underwater Research and Exploration) and is a member of the Eastern Dive Boat Association and American Sport Divers Association. Dan is the author of the original WRECK VALLEY book, a record of shipwrecks off Long Island's South Shore; SHORE DIVER, a diver's guide to Long Island's beach sites; WRECK VALLEY Vol II, a record of shipwrecks off Long Island's South shore and New Jersey; co-author of TROPICAL SHIPWRECKS, a vacationing diver's guide to the Bahamas and Caribbean, BERMUDA SHIPWRECKS, a vacationing diver's guide to Bermuda; publisher of the Wreck Valley LORAN C COORDINATE LIST, co-producer of the WRECK VALLEY VIDEO SERIES and SHIPWRECKS OF GRAND CAYMAN VIDEO. His award winning underwater cinematography has been used on a variety of TV and cable TV shows including CHANNEL 9 NEWS, FOX 5 NEWS, CBS NEWS, CHANNEL 11 NEWS, EYE WITNESS NEWS, LONG ISLAND ALL OUTDOORS, LONG ISLAND FISHING, NEWS 12 and DIVER'S DOWN. Dan's photographs and shipwreck articles have been published in SKIN DIVER MAGAZINE, UNDERWATER USA, NAUTICAL BRASS, The FISHERMAN MAGAZINE, FISHEYE VIEW MAGAZINE, SHIPWRECKS, NAUTILUS, DISCOVER DIVING, WESTERN & EASTERN TREASURES, SHIPS AND SHIPWRECKS plus many more, and he is a contributing editor for the magazine SHIPWRECKS.

v

INTRODUCTION

Wreck diving is a specialized area of scuba diving that can be enjoyed by all divers, in all areas of the world. In the Caribbean islands, traveling tourists can dive and photograph beautiful wrecks in crystal clear waters. These wrecks, as well as many others, for the most part require only standard equipment and scuba skills. Off the east coast of the United States, sport divers visit and penetrate into intact sunken German U-boats, tug boats, destroyers and sailing ships. This type of wreck diving is more advanced, due to the depth and conditions of the water. Depending on the condition of the wreck, location, water conditions, and whether a penetration is planned, special skills and equipment are needed to make the dive as enjoyable and as safe as possible.

Shipwreck diving enables sport divers to visit the past. Each wreck is a time capsule into history waiting to be explored. Sport divers also make interesting artifact finds while exploring the remains of sunken ships. This enables the sport diving community to make its own contribution to historians and archaeologists by giving them the information needed for wreck identification and further research. Within the pages of this book, you will find many helpful hints to make your dives easier and safer. Until now these tricks of the trade have only been learned by years of experience. Realize that no book or article can instantly make anyone an expert wreck diver. Our goal is to give you the needed information and provide a good foundation upon which to build. We will discuss specialized equipment, mental attitude, penetration, methods of research available to all divers, artifact preservation, restoration, modification and much more. You will also learn that the sport of wreck diving is performed on many different experience levels and that each dive is a learning experience for future trips. Hopefully this book will enhance your future adventures by functioning not only as an instructional manual but as a reference source.

MENTAL ATTITUDE

Wreck divers should use some of the rules cave divers have been using with much success for years. If any diver in the team does not feel comfortable with a dive, then that dive should be immediately ended. Staying calm, moving slowly throughout your dive, knowing your equipment, and the location of your back up lights and alternate air source can help to prevent stress. Preventing stress can also come from diving frequently, not being over weighted, making sure all of your equipment operates correctly and familiarizing yourself with the wreck.

A proper positive mental attitude is very important when participating in any wreck dive. If an improperly trained diver were to penetrate a wreck, encountering darkness and stirred up silt, claustrophobia and stress could soon lead to panic. If this situation is not immediately handled with a cool head, the results could be fatal.

Never let peer pressure or greed for an artifact lead you to do a dive beyoud your own capabilities or the initial dive plan. Usually the rule is "If you have any doubt, don't do it". Believe me when I say I've sat on the boat many times when I just didn't feel right about diving conditions, the location, or who I was diving with. As a rule, I try to remain calm no matter what situation arises. This can be difficult at times, especially after seeing an eight

Diver Frank Valenti peers into a hatch on the submarine *Tarpon* off North Carolina. Photo by Jozef Koppelman.

foot shark or finding your first porthole, but remaining calm and in control is mandatory. Staying in control not only avoids panic but assures proper air consumption. After all, dealing with a shark or recovering a porthole is much easier when you're not sucking as hard and as fast as you can just to breathe. Captain Steve Bielenda, a noted northeast wreck diver, once told me that a really good wreck diver has to be disciplined and know when to terminate a dive. Even if he has just found a gold bar, a good wreck diver will leave his treasure on the bottom if his air, or bottom time is used up. It is this type of discipline that is necessary in this highly exciting sport.

HAZARDS

While wreck diving is known to have some hazards, most are easily avoidable. All divers should know how to react if and when they do encounter one of these situations.

Monofilament lines used by anglers cover many shipwrecks. Fishermen constantly return to wrecks because of the amount of aquatic life they attract. Unfortunately for them and us, the wreck also snags many of their rigs, leaving the long strands of nearly invisible mono draped across the site. Although many Caribbean shipwrecks do not have this problem, when diving on the East coast, California or in many inland waterways, divers have to be aware of this hazard. When a diver does get snagged, he has two options depending on what part of his body or equipment is tangled. Usually when dealing in light weight mono, a small tug will snap the line; otherwise, simply take out one of the two knives (always kept sharp) and cut the line. Either way this type of snag should cause no stress at all since divers should break or cut the mono almost as routinely as one ties a shoe lace in the morning. By the way, even better than becoming good at cutting mono is developing a good eye for these thin strands and avoiding them.

Fish nets are less common and usually much easier to avoid. These nets are often easily observed. However, in dark or murky waters, these nets can be very hazardous. This is just one more reason to carry not only one but two razor sharp dive knives. Although I've never been tangled in a fish net, the rule is the same; Stop; Think then Act. Stopping all motion will prevent further entanglement, and if the snag is small, you may try to simply undo it. If you can't, then again cut yourself free with a good sharp knife. Could you imagine how entangled you would become if you tried this with a dull knife?

Entrapment inside a wreck is also a hazard. This can happen when a diver tries to wiggle through a hole that is not large enough for him or he somehow gets lost inside the wreckage. To me this is the worst of the hazards listed so far and requires absolute control, both physically and mentally. Again, Stop; Think then Act. Struggling usually only results in quicker air consumption. If you are stuck, calmly, try to free yourself or signal your buddy to assist you. If you're lost, which should not occur if you are trained properly, use a tether line and do progressive penetration. Try turning off all lights and then look for any ambient light which may lead to an opening large enough to fit through. If your predicament is caused by kicked up sediment and you're at the beginning or middle of your dive, try staying motionless for about one minute. The silt may settle enough to see your way out, but be forewarned that one minute may seem like an eternity.

In 1985, while diving on the wreck of the German submarine *U-853*, my dive partner Billy Campbell and I penetrated through a hole just forward of the conning tower. We started to swim forward, room by room, carefully finger walking so as not to kick up any silt. While moving through a hatch between the 2nd and 3rd room, I found myself stuck. I tried moving forward but was restrained, and when I tried to back out, I was still caught. Now this was a little strange because the hatch was big enough for one diver wearing doubles and a pony bottle, but nevertheless I was stuck. I was in 130 feet of water and three rooms deep into a German submarine. I took a quick glance down, and there in front of me were two shoes and two leg bones, one of the sad fatalities of World War II. At that particular point in time, I thought I was about to panic. Then I caught hold of myself and thought out the situation. First, I checked my air supply; it was fine; next I started to feel for what had me snagged. Bill, who was behind me, saw that I was caught, but couldn't get close enough to help. I could feel that the snag was on my left side and high by my tanks. With one hand, I felt around and found that one of my pressure gauge hoses had caught onto a small pipe. By trying to move forward or backward it would not come free, but by simply leaning to my right it came loose. This whole scenario had occurred and was resolved in less than one minute. It had caused no panic, and my air consumption was still normal. Bill and I turned around and explored more of the wreck as we exited. If, however, this or any number of other situations occurred and the diver in trouble panicked, that diver would be in real trouble. Calm, collective thought is the key to dealing with any hazardous situation.

TYPES OF SHIPWRECKS

Throughout the world, there are shipwrecks of all types and ages. They range from ancient Egyptian vessels and Spanish galleons, which now are often only piles of ballast stone, to luxury liners, oil tankers, airplanes, and barges, even small cabin cruisers. Each is distinctly interesting for many reasons. For example, a barge that we often dive is really nothing but a big hulk of wood on the bottom. There is nothing historical, no artifacts, and the

The tankers Gulftrade (above) and the R.P. Resor sinking after being torpedoed off New Jersey in 1942. Photos courtesy National Archives, Washington, D.C.

water is murky, but she happens to be a great wreck for spear fishing, and we can always find lobsters living between her broken beams. Sport divers will most often find themselves diving on fishing vessels, tug boats, or ships sunk during one of the world wars. Each of these wrecks will differ drastically and will, therefore, have to be approached with a slightly different diving style. As varied as the types of shipwrecks are, so are water conditions surrounding them. If the same tug boat were sunk in Grand Cayman and in New York, the dives would be drastically different due to water clarity, temperature and currents or surge. Aside from location, depth plays a very important role. A tug sunk in fifteen feet of water might be a great beginner dive, but the same tug sunk in 130 feet should be left for the more experienced diver.

As divers explore different types of wrecks, they soon notice that the deeper wrecks are often more intact than the wrecks closer to shore which suffer from the constant pounding from the sea and become broken up and scattered over large areas.

EQUIPMENT

The author climbs aboard the R.V. Wahoo. Photo by Captain Steve Bielenda.

Equipment

The equipment used in wreck diving will vary from location to location. On shallow scattered wrecks, a single tank of air may be sufficient, but on intact or deeper offshore shipwrecks, double tanks, plus a pony bottle may be necessary. Diving in the warm clear waters of the Caribbean may only require a bathing suit, but New Jersey divers often choose to wear dry suits all year round. Take this into consideration as we discuss the equipment needed for wreck diving. The selection of wreck diving equipment is also a highly individual matter. Just remember, we want to stream line ourselves as much as possible in order to reduce drag, permit easier swimming with less fatigue, and eliminate the possibility of becoming snagged.

A wreck diver's equipment consists of the necessary thermal protection for the area, safety equipment needed for depth, and whatever gear is needed to safely dive the plan. For example, if a diver is planning a dive to 100 feet to penetrate into the wreck's interior to take photographs, he will need the proper supply of air which would be accomplished by carrying double tanks. For his penetration he will need a tether line reel, a main light, back up lights, dive knives and most importantly the knowledge and mental attitude to function in an overhead environment. Lastly, he will need his camera gear. All of this equipment must be located so it is easily accessible and will not be dangling, possibly causing the diver to get snagged. Dangling equipment is also more likely to get damaged, and it is certainly not easily located when needed. There are few hard fast rules regarding the location of items such as back up lights and line reels, but all divers should carefully plan where each piece of gear is to be placed. For example, a back up light is useless, unless it can be easily and quickly located even in the worst conditions. I have always been amazed at how ingenious other divers are in the location of such items. Next time you're on a charter boat, take a look around at how each diver's gear is set up. If you see anything interesting, ask how it works or why it's rigged in that manner. Remember, the only stupid question is the one that is never asked.

It's also a good idea to mark each piece of your equipment with your name. This is very important on busy charter boats when everyone has gear that is similar. Marking your equipment also comes in handy when something is lost, so that if found, it can be returned. Let's start now by examining some basic dive equipment and some modifications that are used in this exciting sport of wreck diving.

THERMAL PROTECTION
It doesn't matter what area or type of wreck you're diving, some sort of thermal protection will surely need to be worn. As we all learned in our certification class, water conducts heat away from our bodies 25 times faster than air. Depending on the temperature and depth of the water you're

12

diving in, exposure suits will vary drastically in design, thickness and thermal protection. In the Caribbean, divers may choose to wear a lycra suit or a 1/8 inch short wet suit. Northeast divers prefer 1/4 inch wet suits with hood, boots, and gloves or dry suits. Dry suits also come in many designs and materials. Basically you get what you pay for, so get the warmest proper fitting suit that also fits your budget. It is very important to be warm and comfortable while diving to better enjoy yourself. Note that most shipwrecks look more like huge junk yards scattered across the ocean floor. This wreckage is anything but delicate on exposure suits, especially in the knee area. Bill Campbell, a good friend of mine, started to wear knee pads made from old car tire tubes over his suit. He found that with this simple addition his dry suit, or wet suit, would last twice as long, which saves quite a bit of money over the course of a few years. Another added benefit from these tight fitting flexible knee pads is that they inhibit some air from entering the feet of dry suits. This reduced buoyancy in the foot area allows for easier swimming and a more comfortable dive. Other divers compensate by wearing ankle weights while wearing dry suits. Others go a little further than Bill and wear painters overalls over their suit to protect it from the abrasiveness of the wrecks.

Divers who do repetitive cold water dives in wet suits should try bringing a thermos of warm water and pouring a little into your boots and gloves before your second dive. This trick also works well if your suit has not had a chance to dry from the previous days dive. Dry suit divers who find their arms constantly getting wet should try taping the neoprene wrist seals with electrical tape. Do not use duct tape as it is not elastic and may rip the suit when being removed. I have this problem because my wrists are very small, and whenever I work on an artifact, a small channel on my wrist allows water to leak into the suit. When taping the wrist seals, do not make them too tight or your circulation may be cut off. I also recommend folding the last inch of the tape back into itself. This creates a small pull tap which makes the tape easier to grab and pull off later. This tab is especially helpful if the tape was accidentally wound too tightly and you have to readjust it while underwater. Another common modification is to dry suit hoods. Most divers use a hot nail to puncture and seal a small hole in the back of the hood. This hole allows air that would get trapped in the hood to escape. Remember the hole should be in the upper back of the hood.

MASK

Any mask that fits properly is perfectly suitable for wreck diving. If you are near or far sighted, you may consider one of the prescription masks now available over the counter at almost all dive shops. Since many wrecks are accessible only by boat, divers will find they have to make a variety of different entries to get into the water. For this reason it is advisable to wear the mask strap inside your wet or dry suit hood. In case a wave or dive entry rips the mask off, usually the mask will not have been lost but still held on slightly by the hood.

FINS

A diver's fins are a very basic piece of his equipment, and nothing has to be modified for them to be suitable for wreck diving. However, many shipwrecks are in cold waters where divers are forced to wear heavy gloves or mitts. In this type of environment, it can be very difficult to put on or take off your fins. To make this task a little easier, many divers add a pull tab onto the strap of each fin. This tab can be made from a small length of nylon belt material sewn into a loop over the fin strap, or store bought designs are available in dive shops. The tab allows for easy location and for something easy to grab in order to pull on the fin strap. For divers in warmer waters, the tab will not be appreciated as much, but it will still be an improvement.

REGULATORS

Although there is no one brand of regulator that is recommended for wreck diving, divers who are planning to explore wrecks should make sure that their regulator hoses are streamlined. Route all hoses as close to your body as possible. Depending on the regulator model, this can be easy or may require the use of wire ties or velcro straps. The idea is to reduce the chance of a snag.

Divers should also be able to distinguish between second stages. This is extremely important, especially when using double tanks or a pony bottle. If the second stages were not marked, the diver could easily suck his pony dry while thinking he was using his main tank. There are many methods of identification. One way is to use a different style or color for the second stage or use color coded hose protectors. This can be carried one step further by color coding the corresponding pressure gauge with the same color.

The placement of a pony bottle, octopus or the use of a double tank system with twin regulators is often wasted because divers don't take the time to mount the second stage in a convenient and easily reached, secure location. Having the mouthpiece float behind you or drag in the mud is worse than not having one at all. Not only does such equipment get clogged, but it's also not easily located when needed. Your alternate air sources have to be located around your chest area. In fact, if you were to draw an imaginary triangle from your waist up to your shoulders, your extra second stages should be mounted within it. Each must have a quick disconnect release. This means that you should never store your octopus in a buoyancy compensator pocket because it takes too long to get it out when it's needed. There are a number of quick releases on the market, all available at your local dive shop. If you cannot locate one, use an alligator clip. Attach it to your buoyancy compensator, and then clip the exhaust port plastic into its jaws. This clip will hold the 2nd stage firmly in place, yet when it's needed, the diver only has to pull firmly. Another method is to secure the regulator's second stage to a loop of surgical tubing worn around your neck. There is no searching around for your alternate air source because it's always directly under your chin.

O-RINGS
O-rings made out of silicone are recommended because they have a longer life and are more durable than o-rings made of rubber.

BOTTOM TIMERS
Redundancy is certainly the rule when it comes to wreck diving. Since many wrecks are located in deep water, two bottom timers are mandatory. These timers can be part of another gauge or decompression meter just as long as they are easy to read and accurate. Bottom timers can be mounted on a console, on your wrist or even strapped to the deflator hose of a buoyancy compenstaor, anywhere that it's easily located.

DECOMPRESSION TABLES
Wreck divers are ingenious at combining the functions of more than one piece of equipment. They do this in order to lessen the amount of bulk carried or for ease of location. One of the most common of these adaptations is to install a set of decompression tables inside a clear dive light housing. These tables are easily read while underwater without fumbling around while looking for them in a bouyancy compensator pocket. An added benefit comes from the tables lasting longer because they are not exposed to the marine environment but rather concealed and protected in a dry housing.

MULTI LEVEL DIVE COMPUTERS
Although having a dive computer is by no means mandatory wreck diving equipment, divers have found these compact gauges to be worth their weight in gold. Many types and styles are available. I recommend a meter that in bold digital numbers tells you exactly where you are and how much if any decompression is needed. This information should not have to be interpolated; it should be digital. Personally, I always compute each dive beforehand without the computer. I then make the dive and use the most conservative number. For example, if the multi-level computer tells me it's safe to ascend with no decompression stops, but the dive tables tell me to stop, I make the stop. If the tables say it's OK and the computer says to stop, I stop. I also throw in a five minute safety hang at twenty feet as an extra security measure. I call this computer assisted diving. It is also a good idea to start your dive at the deepest level you want to explore and finish shallower. Remember the dive computer is just a tool; use it wisely, and it will enhance

Dan Berg checks his Beuchat multi-level dive computer
before ascending from a dive. Photo by Jozef Koppelman.

Beuchat Aladin Pro multi-level dive computer. Courtesy
Beuchat. Photo by Daniel Berg.

your enjoyment of the sport. Aside from calculating multi-level diving, the
dive computer is an excellent and extremely accurate bottom timer and
depth recorder. Other benefits of many computers include ascent rate
monitor, surface interval timer, dive log, time before flying, and a repetitive
dive depth no decompression time scroll.

GAUGE CONSOLE

Consoles are very popular in all types of diving. By utilizing a console, a
diver can quickly scan all of his gauges at one time. Consoles range from
small two gauge units to rigs that hold five or six gauges. Consoles can also
provide an easily located spot for mounting a dive slate and back up knife.

GOLVES AND MITTS

In colder waters when gloves or mitts are worn, the abrasiveness of wreck
diving can usually be noticed quickly on the finger tips. After only a few

dives, chunks of neoprene seem to vanish, leaving only cold bare flesh to face the elements. To increase the life of neoprene gloves or mitts, I recommend using a thin coat of Aqua Seal glue on the finger tip area of each glove. Be careful not to apply too much glue, or you will lose dexterity to the stiff hardening substance.

To properly apply, squeeze a small portion onto a paper plate, then with a plastic knife spread the glue onto each desired area. Without any delay, scrape off as much of the glue as possible leaving only a thin abrasive resistant coating. This coating will quite easily double if not triple the life of your gloves.

WEIGHT BELT

The equipment used in wreck penetration is different from any other type of diving. Take weight belts, for example. We have always been taught that a weight belt is an expendable piece of equipment and should be able to be dropped quickly in an emergency situation. Wreck divers who explore the exterior of ships also need to be able to easily drop their weight belts, but when doing wreck penetration a diver never wants to drop his weights. The reason is simple: A diver's weights compensate for the positive buoyancy of his wet or dry suit. If a wreck diver's quick release buckle were to get snagged and released while inside a wreck, he could find himself plastered to the wreck's ceiling. The answer is to install two buckles to your weight belt. Only use the first while outside a wreck, and then before beginning any penetration, clamp the second buckle shut. This will give you the added security needed inside while allowing for an emergency outside or on the surface. Divers should also only attach expendable items to a weight belt. In an emergency, you should not even have to think twice about dropping the belt. A short story comes to mind that will put this in better perspective. I was on a charter boat once when a diver surfaced. He was having a problem because he was over weighted and was having a hard time staying on the surface. Steve Bielenda jumped in, approached the man and yelled at him to drop his weights. He refused and was now gulping for air as he kicked frantically to remain on the surface. Steve's next move was nothing less than brilliant. He said, "Hand me your weight belt and I'll swim it back to the boat for you." The diver quickly released the heavy belt with bug bag and light attached and handed it over. Steve grabbed the belt, pulled it away so as not to catch on any of his gear and released it. Both returned to the boat safely, and the belt was retrieved on our next dive. The moral is that because the diver had his expensive dive light and mesh bag with a two pound lobster in it attached to his weight belt, he was un-willing to part with it even in an emergency situation.

DIVE KNIVES

It is essential for all wreck divers to wear at least one dive knife, and it is also highly recommended to have a back up knife. Almost any manufacturer's

Equipment

Wenoka dive knives. Courtesy Wenoka Sea Style.
Photo by Daniel Berg.

Dennis Lee Berg cuts a rope while exploring
the wreck of the *Mahoney* in the Bahamas.
Photo by Daniel Berg.

knives will do, but bear in mind that you get what you pay for. The first choice is what blade alloy to buy. Stainless steel varies greatly in its strength, durability and rust inhibiting factors. For example, 304 series stainless offers excellent resistance to rust but needs sharpening often and should not be used for prying. 420 series stainless contains less chrome and is less resistant to rust. This alloy is very tough and holds its edge longer then the 304 series. 440 series stainless is a high carbon alloy. Blades made of this alloy will stay sharp for quite awhile. The down side is that the blade will rust and it is a little brittle. Knives made of 440 stainless should not be used for prying. As a main knife, I prefer to wear a medium size blade, solidly constructed with a portion of the blade serrated. This serration allows easier cutting of heavy rope. Other options available in dive knives include ground in line cutters and a solid metal butt on the back end of the handle to use as a tap hammer. I also wear a small sharp back up knife attached to the side of my gauge console. Other divers wear both knives on their legs or mount the back up knife to their buoyancy compensator. As a side note, many wreck divers choose to attach their leg mounted knives with the use of surgical tubing. By doing so, they simply pull the knives up their leg to the predetermined location and do not have to fumble with small buckles when suiting up. Others glue neoprene knife pockets onto their suits. I happen to enjoy the new elastic straps and quick release buckle connections that are now on the market. The main important adaptation that must be performed to some store bought knives is that a wreck diver's knife must be very sharp at all times. This is because in and around shipwrecks, we encounter monofilament lines, discarded penetration lines, anchor lines, and other nets and ropes of all sizes. Each of these could be potentially hazardous if entanglement occurred, and a good sharp knife will assure us an easy escape. A back up knife serves the same function in the case when a main knife is lost or cannot be easily reached.

One way to sharpen your knife is to simply buy a good cross hatched fine metal file from any hardware store. Don't try to get a perfect edge; simply file both sides and leave the ragged razor-like burr on the edge. It's this burr that will slice through rope better than a honed blade. The one down side to sharpening in this manner is that the knife will dull rapidly, so sharpening will be necessary fairly often. I recommend sharpening before each day of diving. Other more sophisticated sharpening methods include honing or stone sharpening.

DOUBLE BANDS

Double bands are available in many different styles and materials. Most serious wreck divers try to get bands made out of stainless steel. These bands are then modified with the addition of a special wing nut, a threaded shaft and a little spot welding so that a wrench is not needed to change the tanks. Another design that I have used for the past few years is velcro double bands. These bands were designed to hold twin 80 cubic foot tanks with a cross yoke bar or anything from 72 to 100 cubic foot tanks with separate regulators. This system is especially nice since one tank at a time can be removed and replaced. The velcro double bands definitely take the struggle out of changing tanks on a boat deck in any type of rolling sea, and pony bottles are easily adapted.

TETHER LINE

A tether line reel is used not only for penetration but as an emergency up line, for search and recovery, underwater mapping, or in the case of limited

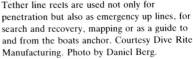

Tether line reels are used not only for penetration but also as emergency up lines, for search and recovery, mapping or as a guide to and from the boats anchor. Courtesy Dive Rite Manufacturing. Photo by Daniel Berg.

Dan Berg using a Dive Rite Inc. tether line reel and NeutraLite 12. Photo by Jozef Koppelman.

visibility, it can serve as a guide to and from the dive boat's anchor. Some divers choose to tie knots in the line every ten feet. By counting the knots as the line is let out, the diver can tell how far he is from the anchor or how deep into a wreck he has ventured. Tether line reels can be home made, converted from construction reels or store bought. Dive Rite Inc., a Florida based cave diving equipment company, offers a complete line of reels. These wreck reels are available with stainless steel construction and contain all of the desired design features such as sufficient line capacity, lock down screw, and contoured winding knob. A reel should always have an adequate supply of line for the depth of water you're diving in. For example, if you're diving in 100 feet of water, your reel should contain no less than 200 feet of line. This is because of the presence of any current when and if the reel is used as an up line. Tether line wreck reels normally use a number 36 white braided nylon line. This line is rated at 350 pounds. Nylon is preferred because it is strong and somewhat abrasion resistant, highly visible and sinks. If a floating line were used, it would have the tendency to get tangled in the diver's feet as it was unreeled, and it would not stay where it was laid out. Tether line reels should never be clipped off and allowed to play out unattended. The reel should be held with one finger firmly on the spool so that the spool turns only when there is tension on the line. When reeling in the line, reel just fast enough to maintain a constant tension on the line. When winding in the line, make sure the line feeds evenly across the spool face to prevent jamming. Remember just having a reel is not a substitute for proper training in wreck penetration.

JERSEY UP LINE

Many wreck divers who explore deeper shipwrecks prefer to mount a Jersey Up Line to their tanks. This 5/16 sisal line is wrapped carefully around a home made reel which is usually about 18 inches long and six or eight inches in diameter. Out of each end protrudes an end of the wood shaft or pipe that runs through the reel. The shaft ends are the diver's handles. Usually a 50 or 100 pound lift bag is permanently attached to the loose end of the sisal line, and the whole unit is attached to the diver's tanks by two strips of elastic cut from a car tire inner tube. To use the up line, the diver reaches back for the lower inner tube strap and pulls it off the bottom handle. He can then grab the bottom handle and pull the Jersey Reel free. The diver then removes the elastic that keeps the line from unwinding, puts a little air into the bag and, while holding both handles, lets the line unwind as the bag rushes to the surface. Note that if the line is not carefully and neatly wrapped, it will most certainly pull out of your hands as the bag ascends. After the bag has surfaced, release some slack then tie the up line to the wreck. Be certain to select a strong spot with no sharp edges. He then cuts the line and puts the reel into a mesh bag and brings the bag with him as he ascends on his own improvised anchor line. This method is excellent because it not only gives the diver a good solid durable ascent line, but the lift bag also acts as a surface marker. Once finished with a safety or decompression hang, the diver can cut the line close to the surface, fold the lift bag and swim back to the boat. If done correctly, the diver will be up current from the boat and can almost drift back. The sisal line that is dropped back onto the wreck is bio-degradable and, therefore, causes no environmental marine problems.

JON LINES

The term Jon Line was first used after a diver named Jon Hulburt, who, while doing a dive on the *Andrea Doria* discovered that decompression hangs in rough water or in a current were made much easier with the use of a short line. This Jon Line is about seven to 15 feet long with a spliced loop at each end. One end attaches to the anchor line by simply passing an end

Divers use a Jon Line to make safety decompression stops easier. Photo by Jozef Koppelman.

through the loop and pulling it snug on the anchor line. The diver or divers (up to three can use the same line) doing a decompression stop can now hang onto the loose end behind the anchor line. In rough water, when the anchor line moves violently up and down, divers using a Jon Line will not find themselves being lifted from their stop depths, but able to maintain their depth relatively easily. Also a much desired benefit of the line is getting the diver out of the crowd. After completing a stop, the hang depth can be easily moved by making a fist around the anchor line just below the snug end and sliding the snug end up. While stage decompression diving is not recommended by any recreational diving agency, this line will also benefit those doing safety decompression stops.

I was first shown the Jon Line while diving the *Coimbra* wreck. We had about 14 foot seas on the surface, but with the use of this easy to make tool, our decompression stops were made more tolerable. One slight modification to the original design is to install a stainless steel locking carabinier to one end. For long stops in a strong current situation, this carabinier can be snapped onto a secure D-Ring on a harness. This reduces arm fatigue greatly.

LIFT BAG

Many wreck divers use lift bags to retrieve objects from the ocean floor. There are many sizes and styles of lift bags, but the most common is an open pillow bag. This means the bag has a small opening at the bottom to allow air to be blown in or expanding air to escape during ascent. This type of bag is carried commonly by wreck divers in the 25 to 500 pound sizes. The most common sizes are the 100 and 250 pound bags because they can be rolled up into a compact size and will lift most artifacts. If an object is found that

The author Dan Berg uses a lift bag to recover a port hole. Photos by Jozef Koppelman.

requires more lift, you can use your buddy's bag in addition and achieve a total lift of 200 or 500 pounds respectively. It is a good idea to use an up line when sending a bag to the surface. This line, which is attached to the bag and the wreck, prevents the bag from drifting away. Divers can use the line from a tether line reel, a Jersey Reel or a Line Ball. A Line Ball is simply a ball of strong line bought in any hardware store. The ball should be wrapped in duct tape with one end of the string allowed to protrude through the center. This string is attached to the lift bag before it is sent up. While the bag ascends, the diver holds the ball as the line, which feeds from the center of the ball, releases. Once the bag is on the surface, the diver lets out some slack and ties the ball to a smooth strong piece of wreckage. Usually each ball contains approximately 350 feet of line, so it can be used on a number of lifts. Line balls are also very compact but are not as strong as using a Jersey Up Line, so they should not be used in rough seas or as an ascent line by divers.

23

GOODIE BAG

Goodie bags or Bug bags, Game bags, Tool bags, and Catch bags as they are commonly called are simply a mesh bag that divers use to carry lobsters, tools and artifacts. Wreck divers should keep their bag wrapped up and closed upon itself when starting their dive. The reason is that an open bag would snag on each and every piece of wreckage you swim over. After you have caught a lobster or found an artifact, you can throw the bag over the back of your legs. The bag is of course also snapped onto the lower portion of a buoyancy compensator or harness. This keeps the bag from dragging. Some divers prefer to use a 1/2 inch rope instead of a harness. The D-Ring rope is approximately two feet long and is spliced into a loop on one end and has a D-Ring spliced on the other end. The rope is attached to the diver's tank valve by placing the loop over the valve before the regulator is attacted. This line which usually hangs over the left shoulder is used to clip the goodie bag. One other note on bug bags, if you are interested in lobsters, buy a bag that has nylon material on the top and mesh on the bottom. This allows you to insert the lobster easily into the bag, without all of his legs getting caught in the mesh.

SNAPS

Most of the equipment divers bring with them has to be attached. Most of the time a brass snap and D-Rings are used. Never use quick spring snaps on your gear. The problem is that these snaps will and do snap onto almost anything as you swim past. For example, I have seen a diver who had a quick snap attached to his weight belt get hooked onto the dive boat's anchor line while descending. Due to the location of the snap and the size of the rope, he could not get it disconnected. I had to cut the webbed belt loop that held the snap to his weight belt. Another time we were shark diving over a shipwreck. A shark cage was floating behind the boat. My job was to film the sharks and to act as a safety diver to the paying customers who were taking turns in the cage. Well, even though we had stated that no one should dive with a quick snap, one girl did. She didn't even get all of the way into the cage when the snap clipped into the wire mesh cage. Again, the diver, her buddy and I couldn't get the snap off, and I was forced to cut through the cage with bolt cutters. Another disadvantage of the spring snap is that it is responsible for a significant amount of equipment loss. For example, if the snap is clipped onto a strap or even a small diameter D-Ring, the snap can be opened unintentionally by twising it so that the spring gate is forced open. Use either stainless steel locking carabiniers or brass snaps with a sliding gate.

LIGHTS

As a wreck diver, you will need two different types of lights and, of course, back up lights. Your main or primary light should be a powerful, dependable

The author Dan Berg using a Dive Rite NeutraLite 12. This light, which has a separate battery pack, was originally designed for cave divers. The powerful beam, burn time and durability make it a natural for wreck diving. Photo by Jozef Koppelman.

An assortment of underwater lights. Photo by Daniel Berg.

wide beam light capable of illuminating the wreck's interior darkness. For penetration dives, this primary light should have a burn time longer than the planned duration of the dive. For any wreck penetration diving, a second wide-beam backup light is also needed. The second type of light is a smaller spot light used to look deep into holes to help you spot lobsters and artifacts. Remember the location of these lights is critical. Each should be located in a secure place that doesn't cause a possible snag yet allows easy access. If your enjoyment comes from lobstering around shipwrecks, try taping a lobster size gauge to a small narrow-beam spot light. This combines two items of equipment and makes it quick and easy to find, catch and measure lobsters without fumbling around for a gauge. Remember, as with night diving, it is important never to shine your light into your own or anyone else's eyes. This would have an immediate negative effect on night vision ability.

Bill Campbell, from New England, with two Super lights mounted to his helmet. Photo by Eva Longobardi.

HEAD AND HELMET LIGHTS

Wreck divers as well as night divers and cave divers have found that having a light or lights mounted on their head allows the divers to have free hands while being able to see. There are all types of helmet lights on the market, or divers can use a little ingenuity and modify almost any light to be head mounted. A friend of mine, photographer, Bill Campbell, from New England, adapted two Modular Super lights to be helmet mounted. These lights, which are a favorite of wreck divers, are all that Bill needs to make almost any dive. My own system is a little less extreme: I use a small Mini C light, which is clipped onto a small piece of neoprene that is glued onto my hood. This setup allows me to have a back up light in a location which is out of the way. The light comes in very handy when I'm engaged in working on artifacts or after I have penetrated a wreck with a main light and a line reel, I then turn around and use the head light to navigate out, allowing both hands to reel in line. One down side to head mounted lights is that while diving in a dry suit, it increases the amount of head movement which can increase the amount of leakage through the neck seal. This problem is usually only temporary until the diver familiarizes himself with movements that don't cause leakage.

When choosing a light to be head mounted, make sure it is easy to switch on. Then decide, based on the type of diving you do, whether you prefer a large main light or a smaller backup light. Cave diving lights are also excellent for head mounting. These units, with remote battery packs mounted on a harness or tanks, are extremely powerful and long lasting.

Dan Berg navigates to a shipwreck, from the beach, with a propulsion vehicle. Photo by Jozef Koppelman.

PROPULSION VEHICLES

Propulsion devices are a luxury to wreck divers. They allow more ground to be covered during a dive and have been used successfully to move quickly to find more productive areas of a wreck. These units are also very useful when navigating to a wreck from the beach or, as is covered in the excavation section of this book, as a digging tool.

FLOATS AND MARKERS

Markers can be store bought or home made. They are very useful in marking the location of an artifact for future dives or in marking the location of a wreck. I have found marker floats very useful in exploring shallow wrecks that can be reached from the beach. After successfully navigating to the wreck and sending up a marker, divers can search the sand surrounding the wreck or do a second dive without having to spend time relocating the site. Painting markers with day glow or fluorescent orange paint will make the markers even more visible.

The author sends up a home made float to mark a wrecks location. Photo by Jozef Koppelman.

TOOLS

While tools are certainly not mandatory for wreck diving, many divers bring tools with them to aid in the removal of artifacts. It's not uncommon for a wreck diver to have a sledge hammer, chisel, and crow bar as part of his standard dive equipment. I only want to bring up these tools to discuss the way they should be mounted. First of all, the weight of each tool must be reduced from the amount of weight on your weight belt, or you will sink like a rock. Remember that losing a tool will change your buoyancy possibly during ascent. The placement of each tool, or in fact, any piece of equipment is critical. Everything must be stream lined and in a location where it is easily found. For example, what good is a back up light if you can't easily and quickly locate it and turn it on? The same thing applies to tools: why bring a crow bar if you can't use it or if your tools constantly drag and snag into each piece of wreckage as you swim by? Some divers attach a foot of line to the handle end of a sledge hammer, clip the loose end to their harness and jump in. This may sound acceptable at first, but once on the wreck, the loose hammer acts as a grapple hook and snags onto any piece of wreckage. Back on the boat, when divers usually feel a little safer, I've watched these hammers swing like a pendulum picking up momentum with each roll of the boat, all the time just missing the unsuspecting diver's knee cap. Remember wreck diving is fun and exciting, but just because someone else dives with a hardware store full of equipment doesn't mean you have to.

When working with tools on or inside a wreck, it is easy to misplace them. It seems like the wreck just eats up sledge hammers and chisels every time you put them down. In reality, the tools usually slide down into a crevice or are hidden by silt. To help to insure against the loss of such items, it is recommended that tools are painted a bright color, like fluorescent orange or yellow. Colored duct tape works just as well and seems to hold up even longer than the paint, especially as the tool starts to rust. Other tools may be kept on the boat until an artifact is found that requires that particular tool for removal. Some of these tools are monkey wrenches, car scissor jacks, hack saws, wedges, drift pins, adjustable wrenches, bolt cutters, and even pneumatic tools. Since many of these tools are quite heavy, most divers choose to bring them into the water only when needed for a particular project. They then transport them in a large tool bag, clipping it to the anchor line and letting it slide down independent of any divers. This system is often used on private boats and only with permission on charter boats, and, of course, it is necessary to make sure that no one is below before the bag is sent down the line. These bags are not attached in any way to the diver, so he should not make any weight belt adjustments for them. At the end of the dive, the tool bag may be sent to the surface with a lift bag, or if the artifact needs more work, some tools may be left hidden on the wreck for the next day's dive. As a side note, air chisels do not seem to work well

Diver Steve Jonassen has his sledge hammer
and chisel neatly mounted on his weight
belt. You will also note the double buckle
weight belt release used during wreck
penetrations. Photo by Daniel Berg.

Dan Berg uses a four pound sledge hammer and
chisel to recover an artifact. Photo by Jozef
Koppelman.

underwater. The problem is that it's hard to keep a forward force on the
tool. Most often the diver moves back rather than the tool digging in.
Hacksaws do work well, with the water acting as a coolant and lubricant for
cutting. One trick is to install two blades in the saw, one cutting in each
direction. This causes the saw to cut a wider slot and avoids binding. Spare
blades can be mounted with duct tape to the top rim of the saw. Always
remember to check your air and breathing rate constantly when doing any
underwater work.

HARNESS

A harness is made of nylon web belt, and its design and construction vary
greatly depending on the manufacture. Most harnesses provide secure
D-Rings for attaching lights, reels and tools. Using a harness is optional and
a personal preference.

29

METAL DETECTORS

Metal detectors have been very popular with treasure hunters for years. They allow these divers to find gold and silver coins plus many varied artifacts buried up to twelve inches below the ocean floor. Metal detectors are also an excellent tool for recreational wreck divers and are rapidly increasing in popularity, especially for use on older wooden vessels. The very first time I ever took a detector onto a wreck, I located a pile of brass spikes and a few pewter toys. During following dives, after spending some time learning how the machines worked, I added some gold and silver to my collection. With some experience, you can determine the approximate size of an object by the tone the detector makes. Usually a small sharp tone means a coin, ring or other small object, while larger tones may mean junk, spikes or large steel objects. With a pulse detector, having a good ear for the deep faint signals will surely be rewarded. A good friend of mine, treasure hunter, Mike McMeekin, continues to tell me that treasure is where you find it, and just like the lottery, you can't expect to win it if you're not in it. If you have never tried an underwater metal detector you're missing out on a lot of fun and possibly some treasure.

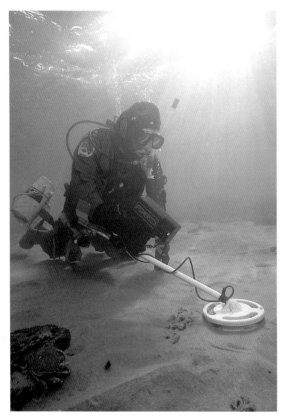

The author scans the sea bed, for buried artifacts and coins, with a Fisher model 1280-X metal detector. Courtesy Fisher Metal Detectors. Photo by Jozef Koppelman.

There are two types of underwater metal detectors and about a half dozen major manufacturers. Motion detectors require the search coil to be in motion in order to locate a target. The unit then beeps as the target is passed. Divers fanning the sand constantly check to see if the target has moved while they dig. The pulse detector does not need motion and will continue to sound a steady tone when held over a target. Both types of machines should be operated by slowly moving the coil, sweeping the sand in front of you. As a side note, if two divers are using metal detectors at the same time, they will have to stay approximately ten to 20 feet apart from one another, or the machines will react to each other causing false readings. Both types of machines work great in the water, but there are other considerations when purchasing a metal detector. Some machines work better in salt water than in fresh. Others are adaptable for beach and land hunting, and others have better volume control for hearing through a neoprene hood. I have used both the Garret Sea Hunter model XL500 and the Fisher Aquanaut model 1280-X and have found them to be excellent machines. With these units, I have consistently retrieved coins, artifacts, gold and silver. Remember that you should never ascend or descend while wearing ear phones. Put the ear phones in place at depth and remove them before beginning your ascent. This will prevent any equalization problems.

DIVE BOATS

Dive boats vary drastically in size, style and design, depending on what type of conditions they were designed for. For our purposes, they will fall into two main categories: commercial and private. When dealing with commercial charter boats, divers should have to check only to see that the Captain is licensed and that the vessel is certified for the number of customers on board. Divers can usually just relax and wait for the Captain to anchor up to the wreck and then enjoy the dive. Private boats, however, need a little more discussion. First, the boat, hopefully a good sea worthy craft, needs to be prepared for diving. Of course, a dive flag is necessary, but so is a grapple hook, granny line, current line, oxygen, medical kit, sturdy ladder, radio, depth recorder, loran C, radar, and compass, as well as the knowledge and seamanship to use them. As with wreck diving, duplication is the key to a safe and enjoyable day. Many boats choose to have two lorans, radios, and depth recorders. Private boats may also have davits to hoist in heavy artifacts and tank racks or bungie systems to prevent damage due to tanks rolling in a heavy sea. Since this book is not about seamanship, rescue or metal shop, let's assume that the boat is properly fitted and the operator experienced. For new boat owners, I recommend a course given by the US Power Squadron or Coast Guard Auxiliary.

Finding the wreck is the next problem. In Bermuda, Florida or other clear water locations, many wrecks are located with the aid of triangulating land ranges. After aligning these ranges, the skipper looks for uncharacteristic straight lines on the otherwise barren sand or coral bottom, which indicate a wreck is underneath. In the northeast, most wrecks are located with a loran C. Loran, an acronym for Long Range Aid to Navigation, triangulates land based radio transmission broadcast from approximate right angles and interpolates this information into two lines of numbers. A loran location is usually exact to within 50 feet, which means that each time you return to the exact number where the wreck is, you are within 50 feet of the exact spot. Loran numbers for known shipwrecks are available in a number of shipwreck books as well as on nautical charts. Boaters should realize that the loran number taken on one boat may be slightly different from the reading observed on their boat. This is why it is very important to keep your own list of loran numbers. When you are doing an initial search for a wreck and have approximate numbers place a marker buoy over the numbers you have then do a series of slow grids over the area. The whole time keep an eye on the depth recorder, watching for the wreck profile. You can also watch for depth changes because it's common for larger wrecks to have wash out around them. If the depth drops quickly, it could be a wash out. Grids can be of circular shape, figure eight or straight line. Once the wreck is located, another marker buoy can be tossed over and the exact loran number should be noted.

To anchor with a grapple hook, simply approach the marker buoy from down-current and toss the hook after the wreck appears on the recorder. The hook should grab in one or two throws, and divers can then descend to tie in the hook. The grapple should be tied into the wreck to prevent it from breaking free. Some divers use a separate line, while others just wrap the grapple hooks chain around some solid wreckage. Be very careful when working with an anchor. Any surge, wave or current can quickly pull the hook upward. Always stay up-current from the grapple when setting or pulling it. Never get between or under the anchor line to work on the anchor. Whoever sets the hook should also make sure that the line cannot chafe on any overhead wreckage. Before sending divers into the water, the boat operator should be certain to raise a dive flag, put a current line with a float off the stern and if there is any current present, he may set up a granny line. Granny lines are used by divers to assist themselves up to the anchor line in current situations. The granny line should be attached to the anchor with a shackle and weighted so it drops to about 20 feet. The line should also be attached to the dive boat's stern, so it is within easy grasp after a diver does his entry. The granny line works well especially when divers are entering the water using a giant stride entry. This is because the diver has

The R.V. Wahoo, a 55 foot commercial dive boat based in Long Island, New York. Photo courtesy Captain Steve Bielenda.

Steve Jonassen prepares to toss a grapple hook over in order to snag into a shipwreck. Photo by Daniel Berg.

The author's 24 foot dive boat, Wreck Valley. Photo by Hank Garvin.

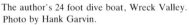

better control over where he is going to land. Sometimes divers using entries such as the back roll will get caught in the floating granny line and have to adopt other techniques. In these cases, divers can be pulled forward by someone on the boat with a short line. There should also always be a capable person left in charge of the boat. Never leave the boat unattended while you go diving. Whoever is left topside should be instructed not to allow any other boats to anchor on top of the divers in the water. He should also know how to operate the vessel, use the loran, have the correct loran coordinates for the wreck and know how to use the radio and the proper emergency channels. Let me stress the importance of this with a little story. Of course, as always I had to learn the hard way. Kevin Travell, a dive buddy of mine, and I were diving a small tug boat, the *Fran S*. It was a night dive, and Kevin had brought our friend Phil to sit on the boat. Phil had never been on my boat before and had absolutely no experience in power boating at all. Kevin and I anchored, then descended, leaving Phil in the middle of the ocean on a dark full moon evening. After catching about six lobsters, Kevin and I checked our air and bottom time. We headed for the bow, and I started to untie the grapple anchor that secured the dive boat to the wreck. Kevin tapped me on the shoulder; he was tangled in some monofilament line. I quickly hooked the grapple back into the wreck and cut the fishing line off Kevin's first stage. When we turned around, the grapple was gone. We came up on an up line, did a safety stop and surfaced to find we were alone, floating in the middle of the ocean in complete darkness. As we rose to the top of a wave, we spotted the boat. Phil was sleeping in the stern while listening to a Sony Walkman. Even if he had heard our whistle, he would not have been able to bring the boat back to us or even use the radio to call for help. I had never taken the time to show him how. Fortunately, everything worked out fine, I took off my tanks and left them with Kevin who was still holding his position with the up line. After what seemed like an eternity I reached the boat and navigated back. We were very lucky, if the current was stronger or if the waves a little bigger, who knows what could have happened.

NAVIGATION

Most wreck dives are done from a boat, anchored above the site. Depending on visibility and currents, it can be at times difficult to find the anchor line once the dive is over. The end result of not returning to the anchor line could be a long surface swim back to the boat or if the diver has exceeded the no decompression limits, a free floating hang. Here are a few helpful hints for navigation around a wreck. First, as with any boat dive, divers should try to start their dive into the current; this will make for an easier swim when returning. If the wreck is intact and the visibility is good, it is often no

The author uses a compass to navigate from the beach to a shipwreck. Photo by Jozef Koppelman.

problem to simply note where you are and return later, but if visibility is limited or if the wreck is scattered over a large area with no distinct reference points, divers can use a tether line reel, clipping one end on or near the anchor while letting line out as they swim to explore the wreckage. This is almost fool proof because as long as the line is not severed, you can easily return to your starting point. Although this is very safe and dependable, this method does have its disadvantages, one of which is the way it limits a diver's investigation to the length of the line, and the same territory must be covered during the second half of the dive. When using this navigational tool, be careful not to let too much line out as you swim. During a visit to the wreck of a German submarine, *U-853*, last year, I watched in amazement as two self acclaimed good wreck divers let yards and yards of extra nylon line escape from their reel. This line drifted into other divers and tangled up an entire area of the wreck. In fact, it was so bad that the divers could not even use the line to find their way back. Aside from not getting any navigational benefit from their tool, these divers ended up cutting the line and leaving it behind on the site. The line would have stayed their for years causing a nuisance to all if it hadn't been cut and removed by two other divers.

The misuse of the tether line is compounded when you realize that this wreck is intact and upright. Submarines are long and skinny. As long as you take note of where the anchor is set, it's almost impossible not to be able to find it, without a line. Each wreck is different, and each diver's capabilities are different. Use these navigational aides when they are needed, and it will enhance your enjoyment of the sport.

Another commonly used method is the perimeter search in which a diver descends on the anchor line and then swims directly to either side of the wreck. The next step is to take note of a unique feature or characteristic and the relative position, then swim up current while exploring, spear fishing, taking photos or whatever is desired. When you want to return, simply swim down current along the wreck's side until you see the same object or road sign. Lastly, swim towards the center of the wreckage where you should be able to find the anchor.

Other methods include attaching a small strobe light to the anchor line about 20 or 30 feet off the bottom. Divers can then freely explore the wreck as long as they remain in site of the strobe light.

After a while navigation becomes second nature; the more dives you do, the better you become. Also, the more dives you do on each wreck, the better the picture in your head becomes as to the wreck's layout. Pretty soon you will recognize parts of the ship and their location in relationship to other areas of the wreck. After many excursions to the same wreck, you will be able to navigate simply from your own knowledge of the area.

If the anchor happens to come loose or you can't find it, you can use your tether line reel, or Jersey reel as an up line. One way to use the reel is to attach a lift bag to the end and send it to the surface. Be sure that your reel is free spinning, or it may pull out of your hands. The line is then tied to the wreck and cut. This method also provides a surface marker and acts as your own personal anchor line. The second method is to just attach the loose end of the reel to the wreck and un-reel the line as you ascend.

Some shipwrecks are located, in shallow water close to shore. Navigation on these wrecks involves how to find them and how to get back to shore when the dive is over. First of all, whether someone has told you of a wreck or you just stumble into one, it is a good idea to take note of its location so you can return. You have to pick at least two objects on the shore at approximately 90 degrees and note how they line up with objects behind them. For example, a telephone pole lines up with the right side of a house, and a water tower's right side just touches a building's left corner. You will note how accurate these ranges are by swimming a few feet in each direction and noting how each range changes. From now on, all you have to do is to navigate to those ranges, descend, and the wreck should be found again. The next step is to take a compass course to your shore entry point and after your dive, navigate to it. Be sure to count each fin kick and make a mental note of the total. I have always found it easier to navigate to a wreck underwater. With the reciprocal of the compass course and the number of kick cycles, you may navigate easily out to the site. Depending on any current and your ability to use a compass accurately, you should swim directly to the wreck. If this fails, you can always surface and use the land ranges before descending again.

Many shipwrecks located close enough to shore for beach dives are popular for night dives and lobstering. When you surface above the wreck at night, many times the shore line with all the street and city lights looks remarkably consistent. The use of a flashing light similar to a road hazard light can vividly mark your exact entry point. This little trick may save a long walk to return to your car.

COMMUNICATION

Underwater communication is discussed in every basic diver's manual and in all certification classes. I'm sure everyone remembers all of the hand signals and the meaning behind each. In fact, in clear water, these signals may work fine, but in the real world of wreck diving, hand signals become very hard to use and understand. For example, if two divers are entering a wreck and the lead diver has a line reel in his right hand and a light in his left, how can he communicate with his buddy. In order to use hand signals, he would have to put down the light or let go of the line reel. If the light was put down, neither diver would be able to see the hand signals, and putting the reel down, which is the direct lead to the entrance, is not a good idea. The divers could use an underwater slate, but again the divers have to stop, put down some gear and one partner may have to hold the light for his buddy. By this time, both divers are kneeling on the usually silty bottom, and the rising sediment is covering them in complete darkness. My partner, Bill Campbell, and I began communicating by talking to each other while diving. There is no trick or any additional equipment needed, just stay close to each other and talk very slowly into your regulator, and keep the sentences short, like, "lets go up," "how much air" etc. In fact, when you first start, try communicating in one syllable words like "up" or "air". If you dive with the same person often, you will quickly start to understand each other. Although Bill and I have used this method during many different types of diving just to avoid the time consuming hand signal and slate methods, its real benefit can be appreciated while on night dives, in limited visibility or while wreck diving. Go back to the original scenario: Both divers could talk to each other while continuing to explore the wreck; they didn't have to stop or put down any of their equipment. It takes a little practice, but it's worth it.

PENETRATION

Penetration is an advanced form of wreck diving. In fact, recreational wreck diving does not typically include penetration. It should only be done by those with adequate experience, training and equipment. The diver who penetrates a wreck must also be disciplined and have a good mental attitude. Penetration is not something you can learn from any book or article or even from years of open water experience. You must slowly approach it through experience and training and evolve into a penetration diver. The techniques and procedures listed below are derived from my own personal experiences. As a disclaimer, they are not nationally approved rules but only one wreck diver's opinions. Each diver is different, and each should use his own good judgment before entering into any overhead environment.

Once inside a wreck, a diver has lost his direct access to the surface. He or she is now in an overhead environment and must use every possible advantage to insure safety. Before I go too far, let's talk about the fine art of entering a wreck. First, if you are using a double buckle weight belt, clamp down on the back-up buckle. Check all of your dive lights to make sure they are still working. If you have excess bulk gear such as a tool bag, or lift bag, you may want to leave it tied near your entry point. This reduces the possibility of snags inside the wreck. Some entries are easy; divers just swim in. Other openings require a few precautions. For example, whenever entering through a vertical hole, enter feet first. This way if you get stuck or just decide not to go in, you can kick to get out. If you enter head first, it is very hard to kick in reverse. It is also a good idea when entering tight holes like deck hatches to keep one arm in and one arm out of the hole. This way if you get caught on something, you have one hand to free the snag.

The key to safe penetration is duplication or redundancy. Hank Garvin, a noted wreck diver, says, "You can't depend on any one piece of equipment except yourself". Start with an air supply of two tanks, a pony, two regulators, two pressure gauges, two depth gauges, up to four lights, two knives and two bottom timers, but the redundancy doesn't stop with your equipment. A diver must be disciplined and know his limits. First, only use one third of your air for penetrating. The remaining two thirds should assure adequate air to exit the wreck and return to the surface. A penetrating wreck diver must be able to find his way out of the wreck. Now we are not talking about a small tug boat sitting in 30 feet of water in the Caribbean. We are discussing a penetration into the dark, broken down, silty remains of a wreck possibly the size of a football field. The diver should always do progressive penetration and slowly extend his comfort zone. This means he slowly learns the area by observation and mental memorization. This may take several dives just to get in past the light zone, but knowing by memory where each bulk head and hatch are in relationship to the exit may come in very handy.

Memory alone is not sufficient for finding the way out of a wreck, especially in an emergency situation when you're under stress. Divers should also use a

Penetration is an advanced form of wreck diving. It should only be done by those with adequate experience, and training. Photo taken on the *Hilmer Hooker*, Bonaire. Photo by Jozef Koppelman.

Memory alone is not sufficient for finding the way out of a wreck. Photo of a cage lamp inside the *Kiysumi Maru*, Truk Lagoon. Photo by Jozef Koppelman.

Diver Dennis Lee Berg peers into the wreck of a small freighter off Paradise Island in the Bahamas. Photo by Daniel Berg.

penetration line. This line should be tied just inside the entry point and again within sight of the opening. The redundancy of tying off in at least two places gives the diver a direct back up in case one knot comes untied or if the line gets cut. Doing progressive penetration gives the diver a back up to his penetration line. The tether line should be unreeled, leaving as little slack as possible. This helps to avoid entanglement in loose line. The second diver in the team should maintain physical contact with the tether line at all times by letting it slide through his open fist. At the end of the penetration, the buddy should turn and exit first while maintaining contact with the line. The lead diver then reels in the line as both divers exit the wreck. A head mounted light comes in very handy when trying to reel and see the way to go.

I remember one dive about eleven years ago; I had penetrated deep into the remains of an oil tanker. At the time I thought I was doing everything correctly. I had bought and used a penetration line and was comfortable that this line would lead me back out. When I was about two levels into the wreck, my line went slack. I immediately realized that at some point it must have been cut, possibly by the sharp ragged edges and rusting steel of the ship. I didn't want to pull the line at all, so I put the the reel down, and we followed the limp line, carefully, not to disturb it. Fortunately the line led to within sight of the entrance. I later found out that another diver had cut the line, without realizing that someone was at the other end. To say the least, the fear that was instilled in me that day has never let me penetrate into any area that I would not be able to find my way out of, even without a line. Remember, redundancy is essential. I have also learned to tie the line or at least wrap the line at several points inside the wreck. These wraps are located at the outer side of bends or away from ragged inside edges and help keep the line from wearing or breaking.

There are all sorts of little tricks wreck divers use to help them navigate inside a wreck. Remember that most wreck penetration is only entering the wreck maybe 20 feet or so. Always take special note of the surroundings. For example, one wreck we dive on lies upside down. By entering the wreck, divers will many times see beams that run on the ceiling below them into the wreck. These beams lead from the entry hole straight into the wreck and can serve as a permanent line for light penetration, as long as the diver keeps in contact with the beam.

Silt and suspended particles are another concern to divers who explore the interiors of wrecks. As a rule, divers usually finger walk or very gently kick, without letting their fins or the fin wash disturb the sediment. One useful kicking method is to have your head down and your feet slightly up. This reduces the amount of floor silt that will be disturbed. Silt can be raised by one fin kick, and even a diver's bubbles can loosen sediment and rust from the ceiling above. The end result is reduced visibility, sometimes to the point of zero visibility. Imagine exploring one room into a wreck with your entry point the only way out when your buddy picks up a porthole and in doing so kicks up the silt. Soon you are in total darkness. Even your powerful dive light won't penetrate through the heavy suspended particles. You put your hand on your mask but still can't see it. What should you do? If you had done everything correctly, the lead diver would have a reel and his buddy would be behind him in contact with the line. Simply carefully reel your way out. If you didn't have a line or if the line snapped right at the worst possible time (Murphy's Law), you could fall back on your knowledge of the area learned from progressive penetration. In situations like this, it is very hard not to get disoriented. Try remaining still for a few minutes; the silt may settle enough to see light, or turn off your dive lights and look for any penetrating ambient light. It may lead out. As with any situation, calm collective thought is mandatory. Panic will lead to disaster.

Wreck penetration divers can and should use a lot of the same rules cave divers do. They are 1) Be trained and dive within your own limitations. 2) Use a tether line and secure it in at least two places. 3) Reserve at least two thirds of your beginning air supply for the swim out. 4) Carry at least three dependable lights. Other cave diving safe practices that are important in wreck penetration are becoming proficient in emergency procedures through practice. Never depend on another's ability to get you in and out of a wreck, know your own limitations. Maintain contact with the guide line. Avoid silt by maintaining correct buoyancy. Avoid passageways where you can not turn around, and remember that anyone can cancel a dive at any time for any reason. A diver should never be pressured into attempting or continuing a dive if he feels fearful or apprehensive.

SHIPWRECK RESEARCH

Wreck research, or the ability to find out pertinent accurate information on a shipwreck of interest, is an important part of wreck diving. It's nice to tell someone that you dove a paddle wheel steamship, but it's downright impressive to show them a historical photo and casually mention the exact date and cause of her sinking. Wreck research can also tie into finding more artifacts or identifying unknown shipwrecks.

There are many sources of information available to the sport diver, depending on the type of wreck and date of her sinking. These range from the knowledge of local fisherman to articles, books and primary source material. Some are more appropriate than others. My basic rule is to take the "easiest path"approach to research. For example, most divers will not want to travel to Washington, D.C., to the National Archives and spend days digging through their card files when a letter can get the same, or sometimes better results. Granted the serious experienced researcher may get more information in Washington, but, in most cases, the pertinent historical information is readily available by mail.

Obtaining the ship's name and approximate date of her sinking are the starting points of most research projects. The ship's name can be found by divers recovering her bell, or capstan cover, or the wreck may be known by a certain name, but her history may never have been traced.

I usually start my research by writing to one or more of the local marine museums. If the wreck is a Naval vessel, I also write to the Navy. If it's a Coast Guard vessel, I'll write to the Coast Guard. If the wreck is a foreign ship, I'll try writing to a marine museum in that country, or I'll hire a researcher overseas to assist in the search for information. While waiting for them to reply, I pay a visit to a nearby library that carries THE NEW YORK TIMES or any local paper on microfilm. THE NEW YORK TIMES is a valuable source of information for the late 1850's and early 1900's. Almost all major shipwrecks are listed on the newspaper's front page or under titles such as marine casualties, explosions, disasters, or shipping. Once at the library, the search can go in either of two directions. If I know the actual date of sinking, I simply ask for the correct microfilm reel and search by page on that date. If the exact date of sinking is unknown, I refer to the index volumes.

These volumes are a little confusing, but contain a wealth of information. Wrecks can actually be found under a variety of sub-titles such as explosions, marine disasters, shipping, etc. Each year they may be listed under a different title, so you must scan all possible subtitles in each volume to find where they have listed shipwrecks in that volume. Once the wreck in question is found, the index gives you the date, page number and column number. This can then be easily found on microfilm. Photocopies can be made of all pertinent pages. Be sure to scan the following day's paper for continuous coverage.

The third source is articles that have been written in either diving or fishing related magazines. These seem even more valuable when you consider that someone else has already gone through the trouble of doing the research. Don't forget to look in any books that may have been written on the particular subject you are studying. There are many well researched books with invaluable information available at local libraries or through dive shops. Last, but not least, talk to divers who frequent the area. Diver learned knowledge is vital to all research projects. They can give you valuable information such as depth, condition, layout, aquatic life, types of artifacts and currents.

By the time you're done, I'm sure you will have a folder full of photo copies from different sources. No doubt you will also have conflicting information as to the time, date and number of casualties. What I've found to be the causes are typing errors from the original articles printed about the wreck. These articles with bad information become a source of information for the next author who is writing on the same subject, and thus creates a vicious cycle. As a researcher, you are responsible to be as accurate as possible. Usually going back to your earliest source for verifying information assures accuracy. If available, check out any conflicting information by going back to the original Coast Guard or Life Saving Service reports. These are available at some marine museums.

Once finished, share your knowledge with the sport divers in your area. It will make wreck diving more rewarding and enjoyable for all.

SOURCES OF SHIPWRECK INFORMATION

Library of Congress
Geography and Map division
Washington, DC 20540

Mariners Museum Library
Newport News, VI 23606

Maritime Administration
Division of Reserve Fleet
Fleet Disposal Branch
Department of Commerce Building
Washington, DC 20230

National Archives and Records Service
Attention: NCRD
8th and Pennsylvania Ave, MW
General Administration
Washington, DC 20408

National Maritime Museum
Porter Shaw Library
Foot of Polk Street
San Francisco, CA 94109

National Ocean Service
Hydrographic Surveys Branch
6001 Executive Boulevard
Rockville, MD 20852

Naval Historical Center (SH)
Building 220-2
Washington Navy Yard
Washington, DC 20374

Peabody Museum of Salem
Phillips Library
East India Square
Salem, MA 01970

Philadelphia Maritime Museum Library
321 Chestnut Street
Philadelphia, PA 19106

Smithsonian Institution
Museum of American History
Washington, DC 20560

Steamship Historical Society of America
University of Baltimore Library
1420 Maryland Ave
Baltimore, MD

South Street Seaport Museum
207 Front Street
New York, NY 10038

Texas Antiquities Committee
Box 12276
Capitol Station
Austin, TX 78711

GREAT LAKES

Burton Historical Collection
Detroit Public Library
5201 Woodward Ave
Detroit, MI 48226

Dossin Great Lakes Museum
Great Lakes Maritime Institute
Belle Isle
Detroit, MI 48207

Great Lakes Charts
630 Federal Building
U.S. Courthouse
Detroit, MI 48226

Great Lakes Historical Society
480 Main Street
Vermilion, OH 44089

BERMUDA

Bermuda Maritime Museum
Po Box MA 273
Mangrove Bay, Bermuda MA BX

CANADA

Canadian Hydrographic Service
Surveys and Mapping Branch
No 8 Temporary Building
Ottawa, Ontario, Canada

Wheelhouse Maritime Museum
222 Cumberland Street
Ottawa 2
Ontario, Canada, K1N 7H5

Public Archives of Canada
Trade and Communications Records Center
395 Wellington Street
Ottawa, Canada, K1A ON3

ENGLAND

Imperial War Museum
Lambeth Rd
London, England, SE1 6HZ

National Maritime Museum
Greenwich
London, England, SE1 9NF

Cunard Museum
University of Liverpool
Po Box 147
Liverpool, England, L69 3BX

SPAIN

Archives Of The Indies
Seville, Spain

Museo Naval
Madrid, Spain

Museo National
Madrid, Spain

SHIPWRECK IDENTIFICATION

Identifying an unknown shipwreck is no easy task and there are no easy to follow rules. The most positive identification is only made through the retrieval of artifacts from the wreck, but even this seemingly foolproof method can deceive the most learned researcher. I'll describe some past experiences. All of these wrecks are off the south shore of Long Island, N.Y.

While researching information for a previous book, WRECK VALLEY, I tried to find information on a local lobster wreck called the *Fire Island*

Gary Gentile, author of the book ADVANCED WRECK DIVING GUIDE, with a bell he recovered from the World War II freighter *Manuela*, North Carolina. Photo courtesy Gary Gentile.

Diver Rick Jaszyn holds the bell he recovered from the *Durley Chine*. Photo by Hank Garvin.

Captain Steve Bielenda holds the capstan cover that led to identification of the freight steamer *Kenosha*. Photo by Daniel Berg.

Mike DeCamp holds a plaque he recovered from the *Varanger*. Photo courtesy Mike DeCamp.

Lightship. I found two reference books that listed her sinking due to a collision, but after diving the wreck, I knew something was wrong, and I could not simply duplicate an error in my book. Since diving the site, I knew that this low lying wood wreck could not possibly be a steel hulled lightship but was an unidentified wreck named, possibly by fishermen, for her location near the old lightship station. I researched and found that although the lightship had been in a collision, she had never sunk. A few years later, we dove her again and a friend, Mark Weiss, brought up a bronze windlass cover. On it was the name "*Madagascar*". We all assumed that the identification process was over. We were wrong because I could find no record of a ship called *Madagascar* sinking in our area. After a few weeks and after calling in a few favors from a friend at the National Archives in Washington, D.C., I found out that the *Madagascar* had changed names, and the wreck we knew as the *Fire Island Lightship* was really a freight steamer named *Kenosha*.

On another wreck which had long been known as the *Good Gun Boat*, a diver, Billy deMarigny, found a brass bell which bore the name "*Tarantula*" on it. When I went to research this wreck, I knew her name and approximate age, and I also knew she was armored. I conveniently found a *Tarantula* built for Vanderbilt which had been converted during World War I to a gun boat in the Canadian Navy. I then came across and purchased a beautiful topside photograph, wrote an article about the wreck and was about to deliver the text to the printer when luckily I decided to check just a little deeper. In no time at all, I found that the *Tarantula* I was researching had never sunk; she was still in dry dock in Canada. The wreck turned out to be another vessel named *Tarantula* also built for Vanderbilt and converted during the war by the U.S. Navy into the *USS Tarantula*. It definitely doesn't pay to take any short cuts or to make any assumptions.

On one more site, the *G&D* wreck, I was led astray once again. By checking shipping records and a location given by newspaper articles, I was told by a respected researcher that this was almost certainly the wreck of the *Durley Chine*. Two years later, diver, Rick Jaszyn, found and recovered the bell of the *Durley Chine* on another wreck miles away.

When trying to identify a wreck, first try to gather as much information as possible from local divers or historians. Diving the site and recovering artifacts can be very helpful especially if the object retrieved, like a bell or windlass cover, has the ship's name on it. Otherwise, objects found could be related to a ship's cargo or the age of the vessel, but it is difficult to establish this. I recommend diving as often as possible. Finding the first clue may take years, but once found, it's an invitation to open a time capsule which could have otherwise perished.

FINDING NEW WRECKS

Finding a virgin shipwreck is a dream of all wreck divers. Many wrecks have been located by divers just exploring new areas or checking out new loran numbers supplied by local fisherman. The method of search is as varied as the type of vessels that sail the sea. Most successful searches, however, start with a lot of thorough research. Then, when a likely area is derived, the remains can be located with machines such as side scan sonars or proton magnetometers or less expensive equipment like a depth recorder or the affordable new three dimensional sonar. Other shallow clear water search methods include towing a diver on a sled while the boat does a grid of the area. This method is affectionately called, "towing shark bait". Aerial surveys can also be very helpful, using aircraft, helicopters or even a hot air balloon as Edna and Teddy Tucker did in Bermuda to locate many old wrecks. Aerial surveys should be done no higher than 500 feet. Polarized sunglasses are important as is a good calm day with little surface chop.

Getting back to the more scientific methods, let's first discuss side scan sonar. First of all, these units are very expensive, so they are not common place in the sport diving community. Some are owned and operated by treasure hunters, and these machines are worth their weight in gold. Basically, most side scan sonars use a tow fish which is towed behind the boat at a determined depth. The fish contains transmitting circuitry that sends out high frequency bursts of acoustic energy which project along the

Proton Magnetometer being lowered into the ocean. Photo courtesy J.W. Fisher. MFG.

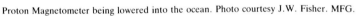

Side Scan Sonar image of the *Henry Holmes* wreck, a cable ship sunk off St. Lucia.
Courtesy Klein Associates, Inc.

Joe Koppelman (left) and Dan Berg with portholes recovered after finding a virgin shipwreck. Photo
courtesy Dan Berg collection.

sea bed on both sides of the boat. Any object that is not buried, like a shipwreck, or other topographic feature on the sea bed produces echoes which are received by a transducer. This information is often computer enhanced to give a detailed image of the wreck. Side scan sonar requires an experienced operator.

Proton Magnetometers, which are considerably less expensive, measure the strength of the area's magnetic field instead of looking for topographic features. The earth's magnetic field is changed locally by the presence of any ferrous object, like the steel in a shipwreck. The amount of change is proportional to the amount of ferrous iron. These machines, which also utilize a tow fish, can find any ferrous metals such as cannons, hull plates, and anchors, even when they are buried beneath the ocean floor. Magnetometers can find wrecks, depending on the amount of iron content, up to 1,000 feet away.

Remember, before buying any expensive equipment or spending days on the boat searching an area, do your homework. Research can narrow the search area down and save countless hours of wasted time.

MAPPING

In discussing mapping with sport divers, it becomes apparent that most do not have the means or ambition to do a scientific grid or even run a datum line. Sport divers do, however, want to contribute and are very capable of producing a complete or partial wreck map based on diving observations, experience and even memory.

Any knowledgeable shipwreck archaeologist should realize that recreational sport divers are a great and valuable source of information. With the limited number of archaeologists as well as limited funding, they could never hope to cover even a small percent of known shipwrecks. Therefore, the sport divers who are out there diving every week end exploring all types of sunken vessels develop a wealth of information, and, in using this information, wrecks can be better understood.

I try to draw a wreck after only diving it once. This drawing may be of a small area or a rough outline with only very distinct features crudely drawn in. Then after additional dives, I add and change details as I become more familiar with the wreck. I've found this very unscientific method to be quite successful, especially because recreational divers don't need to know where every brass pin is located. We only need a basic wreck drawing to help each other to understand the wreck's layout.

Mapping

In addition to drawing from memory, I can now look at photographs of a wreck and make changes or add more detail to my drawing. Underwater videos have recently become affordable to many divers. These housings with wide angle lenses containing 8mm, Hi 8, super beta or VHS format camcorders can accurately record all images viewed during a dive which can later be seen at home. When using the video, try to take the footage from the same angle that you want to draw the wreck. Then swim along the side very slowly. Depending on the size of the wreck and the visibility, it may take a few passes to capture all the details on film. The tape can then be viewed at home and details can then be added to the wreck map. Both the camera and especially the video are excellent tools and will produce great results as well as increased accuracy.

The purpose of doing a wreck drawing can be varied. Maybe you want to display your work in a local dive shop, or next to a prized artifact, or maybe you realize that others can benefit from your efforts. Imagine being able to show a new diver a drawing of the wreck he is about to dive on; he could then descend and recognize the different areas. It would also make dive planning a lot easier, knowing the depth of a portion of the bow, or the distance from the pilot house to the stern. Underwater photographers wouldn't have to rely on chance or luck to find those dramatic wide angle shots. They could plan out shots by looking at a sketch of the wreck just before jumping in.

Diver using a camcorder and Amphibico video housing to accurately record the layout of a shipwreck site. Photo by Daniel Berg.

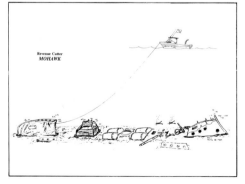

Sketch of the *Revenue Cutter Mohawk*, which was sunk off Long Island, New York on October 1, 1917. Sketch by George Quirk and Daniel Berg.

LAWS

In recent years archaeologists have fought to restrict divers from diving on and removing artifacts from shipwrecks. New laws have been passed to protect historically significant wrecks and I'm sure we can expect additional legislation. The underwater archaeologist contends that recreational divers and treasure hunters destroy shipwrecks and sometimes do not preserve the artifacts they recover. They want to have control over all wrecks and then limit our access to them. In fact, I was recently told by the director of a marine museum in Bermuda that he could not supply me with any historical information because he did not want recreational divers to dive wrecks. My feelings on this subject are very strong, so without going into detail, I would like to say that many museums have also left their historically significant artifacts to decay without any presevation, and many archaeologists are presently working on shipwreck sites that were originally located by recreational divers or treasure hunters. I also believe that leaving an artifact on a wreck does not insure its survival. For example, I have seen objects which unfortunately I couldn't get close enough to retrieve such as portholes and china bowls get crushed after a storm or corrosion collapsed a bulk head. I also feel that treasure hunters and recreational divers are an invaluable source of information. These divers are in the water every weekend and know not only the location and layout of many wrecks but were also responsible for their identification. Archaeologists do not have the funding or time to explore all of the shipwrecks sport divers regularly dive on, and I hope that the two sides can one day work together rather than against each other. Anyone who recovers an artifact should only do so if he is willing to preserve that artifact. Divers should also display their treasures for all to see and enjoy. Displays can be set up at local museums, libraries, and dive shops.

Before removing artifacts from a wreck, please check the salvage laws and antiquity protection laws in your area. Each state may have different laws pertaining to the recovery of artifacts that fall into the antiquity classification. Many times a sunken vessel may not be legally abandoned by the owner. Removing artifacts would be illegal. Believe me, it is important to be knowledgeable in local laws before salvaging a shipwreck.

ARTIFACT LOCATION

Although many divers simply rely on what they happen to see while diving, there are a few things that a diver can do to hedge the odds at finding nice artifacts. Didn't you ever wonder why the same divers always find the portholes or bring up silverware or china? It's no trick, but the odds are stacked in his favor over yours. First, he probably has numerous dives under his belt, giving him trained eyes. Plus, after finding a good productive spot, he constantly returns to this spot time after time. For everyone else, it's hit or miss. Well here are a few hints that will give you a better chance. First, always listen very closely to the stories other divers tell, especially if they are willing to give you an area to look in. Second, be very observant of shapes as you swim over or through a wreck. Third, don't expect to be able to pick up and swim off with every great artifact you spot; many will require several dives and specialized tools as well as determination to recover. Fourth, metal detectors are great for finding small objects buried in the sand. Last, but certainly not least, be persistent. If you have located a porthole or a cage lamp or some other nice find but you can't retrieve it, plan on returning to the wreck in the near future. Plan your removal procedure during your surface time. Sometimes a little determination can be very rewarding. These four helpful hints may seem overly simple, but they will produce consistent results. Before I give some examples, I'd like to remind you that the more you dive, the better your chances are of finding and recovering historical artifacts.

An example of how rewarding listening to other divers can be is evident in the following anecdote. In 1986, Captain Steve Bielenda, who runs the R.V. Wahoo, told me how he found three intact bottles on the *Lizzie D* Wreck, during a charter the previous day. This interested me greatly because the *Lizzie D* was a prohibition Rum Runner sunk in 1922, and for years local divers had considered her to be picked clean. After getting off the phone with Steve, I called my dive buddies, and the next morning we were anchored over the wreck. During the previous three years, I had been on this wreck maybe ten times and never found anything but an occasional lobster. On this dive, by digging around the spot where Captain Bielenda had found his bottles, we discovered over thirty intact prohibition whiskey bottles. There were three different styles, and five of them still contained booze. We would never have found any of these if I hadn't listened and learned from another diver.

Being overly observant also pays off. I once watched about twelve novice wreck divers swim over the same area of a wreck, then Rick Schwarz came by, slowly scanning the rusting hulk for shapes and brass. He picked up a brass cage lamp plus a four pound lobster after everyone else had raced over the seemingly barren area.

Determination, as I mentioned before, pays off in the end. Back a few years ago, in August of 1985, Bill Campbell and I were diving around the stern of

A brass porthole. Photo by Keith Wipprecht.

Diver recovers a porthole from a wreck off New England. Photo by Bill Campbell.

Dan Berg (left) and his brother Dennis with portholes recovered from a tug boat wreck off Far Rockaway, New York. Photo by Rick Schwarz.

the *USS San Diego* wreck. As we swam into a wash out, I noticed some brass that was almost completely covered by sand. We both dug it out and were pleased to discover it was the backing plate of a porthole. In other words, it was missing the glass swing plate and brass storm cover. Bill swam away, but I decided to lift it, figuring if I ever found a swing plate off the *San Diego* I'd have a nice artifact. Unclipping a 250 pound lift bag from my buoyancy compensator, I quickly rigged a line and started to fill the bag. Much to my surprise, this started a two year ordeal.

As the lift bag filled, I was amazed at how little my artifact moved. In fact, it hadn't moved at all, and the bag was now overflowing with air. I signalled Bill, who quickly came over and offered his 250 pound lift bag. Within minutes, Bill's bag was rigged, and we found the sand under us starting to move. The rim (a piece of brass weighing no more then twenty pounds) was still firmly attached to a huge steel plate weighing somewhere between 300 and 400 pounds. We sent the whole thing up tied to an up line, which is a line tied to the bag, and then attached to the wreck. This prevents lifted artifacts from drifting away during a diver's ascent and safety decompression hang. When Bill and I climbed back aboard the Wahoo, the normally friendly crew informed me that my up line had snapped, and the mate had to take a swim to secure a line to my drifting bag. They proceeded to tell me that it took five of them to haul it onto the Wahoo's swim platform and I now owed them all a drink. This was a good deal considering the fact that I still needed help getting this huge piece of steel into my truck.

Once at home, I began to separate the porthole rim which was still firmly bolted to solid steel. This in itself was no easy matter, and after many nights of pounding, prying, and chiseling, I realized I was getting nowhere. The owner of a local gas station came to my assistance and managed with the use of his air tools to loosen the brass bolts which had been threaded directly into the armor plated steel. I returned home and stored the rim in my backyard while waiting to recover the missing parts.

During my next few visits to the wreck, I covered as much ground as possible. While swimming along the outside of the hull on one dive, I found what I was looking for: an intact porthole, and the glass was not even cracked. All I had to do was find a way into the wreck, drive the hinge pin out, and the porthole would be freed. I swam aft and found an opening that led into the admiral's quarters. This was an area heavily trafficked by sport divers, so I couldn't imagine how a porthole would remain untouched. After penetrating the wreck, I followed a row of porthole openings and then came to a wall. Since I thought I had gone too far anyway, I went back, dropped down to the next deck, and did the same thing. Still I saw no sign of any intact glass. Retreating once again and swimming up two decks to repeat my

The author holds a brass porthole he recovered from the *USS San Diego* after fifteen working dives. Photo by Steve Bielenda.

procedure, I still found no sign of this elusive treasure. Now, out of time and running low on air, I exited the wreck and cruised back over the porthole. It was a mere fifteen feet from the admiral's quarters opening, but was somehow hidden inside the wreck's rusting interior.

Two weeks passed by before I was able to return to the *San Diego*. This time I measured the distance from the porthole to the opening by counting body lengths. This was repeated on the inside of the wreck with no better results than two weeks earlier. On the second dive of the day, I approached my dilemma a little differently. From the outside of the hull just above my artifact, I noticed a corroded hole, about the size of a dime, through the *San Diego's* outer hull. With a sledge hammer and a chisel, I proceeded to enlarge this hole to about the size of a fist, and then once again, I penetrated the interior, not looking for the porthole, but for the location hole. When I found it, I knew what had gone wrong. Due to the angle at which the wreck is resting, and the amount of silt and debris piled up, much of the interior wall is buried. I had been swimming over it without ever knowing. On the next visit to the wreck, I dug out enough debris to see the top rim. Fortunately, because the *San Diego* is upside down, the hinge pin was located on top and within easy reach. With a sledge hammer and drive pin, I soon found that there was absolutely no room to work. Right next to the rim on both sides were steel beams preventing any type of hammer swing. By this time I was frustrated, but still very determined. I studied the size and shape of the rims hinge at home, and designed a metal pin pusher that could drop over the rim and, by means of a bolt and rachet wrench, drive out the pin while still working within the confined quarters determined by the beams. Over the winter, I made up this new device and eagerly waited to reap its benefits. "Mind over matter," was my new motto. This, of course, didn't even come close to working. My dive buddy, Rick Schwarz, almost died of laughter as he watched my engineering masterpiece crumble in my hands. The hinge pin didn't even have the courtesy to slightly budge from position.

Once again I planned to retrieve the porthole. This time I welded a small drive pin to a long crooked handle made from a bent shaft. The idea was that the drive pin could be held in position with my left hand out of the way and hopefully leave enough room for me to take small taps with a hammer. Although this new tool was made and had been stored with my dive gear, for one reason or another it wasn't used until the summer of 1987.

I had gone on a diving vacation to Bonaire with my wife, Denise, and when I returned, Captain Bielenda informed me that while I was away, a group of divers had located a storage room in the bow of the *San Diego* that was filled with china dishes and that some beautiful pieces had been brought up. He was now running special dive trips to the *San Diego* and anchoring above the china hole, so I signed up for as many trips as possible. On one trip we anchored in the stern, and, since I didn't feel like swimming to the bow because of a very strong current, I decided that is would be the perfect time for one last try at that stubborn porthole. Five minutes into the dive, I had dug out a pit which exposed the top half of the frame. After fifteen minutes, the hinge pin was out, and I thought to myself, this is too easy. Deciding to wait until the second dive, I ascended to the Wahoo and impatiently waited out my surface interval. I proudly boasted to all on board that it should only take another ten minutes of bottom time for my lift bag carrying a porthole to hit the surface. After a three hour interval, I suited up and was all ready for a nice easy retrieval. After doing a giant stride entry, I immediately realized that this was not to be the case. Sometime during my topside time, I had managed to slice a big hole in the left shin of my dry suit, and was flooded with ice cold water instantly. Once again I was left with nothing to show for my efforts. All of the following week, I was concerned that anyone else who dove the wreck could easily recover what I had worked so hard for. On Thursday when I returned, the Wahoo was anchoring in the bow, so divers could head to the china room. This was great for everyone else, but I had to go to the stern which was 450 feet up current. With a propulsion unit in hand I calculated five minutes to travel astern, another fifteen minutes to remove and send up my lift bag containing the swing plate, and then five more minutes to return to the bow and ascend on the anchor line. All went as I had planned. Within four minutes I had my hand on the swing plate, but the only problem was that it wasn't moving. Digging down in the mud, I found two bolts (dogs) securing the swing plate closed. Although I was able

The author Daniel Berg searches the wreck of the *Caesar*, a English brig sunk in 1818, with a Garrett Sea Hunter XL500 metal detector, Bermuda. Photo by Mike Burke.

to quickly loosen them, it still wouldn't budge. Removing my crow bar from its mounted position on my back, I tried to pry it loose. Twenty minutes later, after digging more debris away and breaking the seal, all my efforts were finally rewarded. As I climbed back onto the Wahoo, I anxiously asked if my lift bag had come up. Don Schnell, who was the first mate, supplied the answer by pointing. About 500 feet away was my yellow lift bag, floating high in the calm sea. Even on the surface, this porthole was giving me grief. Exhausted from all the hard work, I had to jump in the water once again and retrieve my lift bag.

With more than fifteen dives tied up in one artifact, I asked myself if it was worth it? I can only answer that by saying that I found another intact porthole on the *San Diego*, and I am now in the process of devising a plan for retrieval. I can only hope that this one will be a little easier!

A few years back, a local diver brought me to a luxury yacht wreck. He had worked the site for some time and considered it to be picked clean. The wreck sat upright and intact in only 30 feet of water. On my first dive, I recovered a porthole. On subsequent dives, Rick Schwarz, Steve Jonassen, Bill Campbell and I recovered over 18 portholes as well as assorted cage lamps and ceiling lights. The reason for our success was the method used to locate the portholes. The divers who had been to the wreck before us had probably entered the wreck and then searched each room for portholes. We did just the opposite. Our divers searched the wreck's exterior. When we found a porthole, one diver would shine his light through the glass, and the other would enter the wreck in search of the light. We found portholes inside closets and behind electrical panels. After completely searching the exterior, Steve Jonassen even found a spare porthole which had been stored in a cabinet.

EXCAVATION

Many artifacts lie buried under sand or mud. These can be found through excavation. Here are a few affordable methods that sport divers can use to work a site.

HAND FAN

The first is my favorite method because it's cheap, easy to make, can be carried on every dive and without too much effort produces fine results. It's

Hand diggers are easy to make and without too much effort can produce fine results. Photo by Jozef Koppelman.

a hand digger or hand fan. Divers can use any number of designs from a ping pong paddle that was first used by treasure hunter, Teddy Tucker, in the 1950's to my own design. My digger is made from a curved piece of 1/8 plate steel, stainless if it's available. Then a piece of 1 inch pipe has a hack saw slot cut through one side. The steel, which can be curved by bending it around a 4 inch diameter pipe, is pressed into the slot. A spot weld assures security between the two components but is not necessary. The finished item can be clipped onto a BC weight belt or carried in a mesh bag. It's held in the palm and can be used to dig or gently fan silt or sand. By always digging in the same direction the current will usually carry any sediment away, leaving decent visibility in the hole. The curvature of the digger's blade allows more material to be moved with less effort and reduces drag on the back swing.

AIR LIFT

An Air Lift is one of the nicest excavation tools. It can be made with pvc, stainless or aluminum pipe and hooked to a suitable compressor will move large volumes of sand with minimal loss of visibility, that is, of course, if it's set up and used correctly. The components of an air lift are simple: a high volume air compressor, a length of pipe, a nozzle and a hose. The unit is built so that a hose connected to the compressor is connected to the bottom of a twenty foot long 6 inch diameter pipe. Other pipe diameters and lengths

An Air Lift can move mountains of sand quickly and efficiently. Here treasure hunter, Carl Fismer is excavating a buried shipwreck in the Florida Keys.
Photo's courtesy Carl Fismer and Robert Knecht

can also be used, but the example used would require 75 psi and 100 cfm of air to work efficiently at 65 feet. A valve is usually located at the bottom of the pipe and allows the operator to control the volume of air being pushed into the pipe. The air lift works because air is forced through a hose to the lower end of the pipe. This air then rushes up the pipe towards the surface, causing a vacuum effect which causes sand, mud or small rocks to be sucked up the pipe. If the lift is set up correctly, the debris will fall down current and heavy objects will not fall on top of the diver working the lift. To better avoid the dumping of lifted materials back onto the divers, a long horizontal pipe can be floated at the surface. Depending on its length, a water jet may have to be used to facilitate the movement of material.

WATER DREDGE

A water dredge can be useful if an airlift is not available. It's made from a high volume water pump, a length of tubing, and hose. The design is similar to an airlift except water is forced into the bottom and directed back up the pipe, thus causing the suction needed to vacuum the bottom. The water dredge may not be quite as effective as an air lift, but, in shallow water up to 35 feet, it works quite well and is easily controllable. Treasure hunter, Carl Fismer, recommends facing into the current when working a water dredge, this way the current carries suspended particles away and allows good visibility for the diver.

Treasure hunter, Carl Fismer uses a Water Dredge to work a shallow water wreck site. Photo courtesy Robert Knecht, by John Berrier

The author Daniel Berg uncovers a cannon from an English warship by digging with a propulsion vehicle. Photo by Jozef Koppelman.

PROPULSION VEHICLE

Using an underwater propulsion vehicle as a excavation tool is not exactly a scientific or manufacturer approved method, but since these devices have become affordable, they have not only helped divers to get to where they want to go but also fan away the sand in order to search for artifacts. By turning a propulsion device away from you while holding its front end against your chest and the propeller pointed down, a diver or team of divers can dig a large hole very rapidly. I prefer to use a model with an adjustable pitch propeller. This way I can run on a low speed. Otherwise, as learned from experience, instead of digging a hole, the diver is simply propelled backwards. Two divers working as a team is the best way to use this method. As a word of caution, this equipment was never designed for this function. Mud, sand and dirt could get caught in the trigger mechanism, causing the unit to stay on. Install a pin that can be used to pull the trigger out in case of binding. If the unit does jam in the on position, you can aim it downward so that it runs itself into the bottom, allowing time to pull the trigger to the off position. Another good idea is to secure the propulsion unit to the wreck, so it can't swim away if the trigger does get stuck. If the unit is secured correctly, it will also reduce the effort of holding it in place and, therefore, reduce your air consumption.

MAIL BOX

The Mail Box or Prop Wash method of excavation is best left to professional salvage divers. Home built units used on small boats will work in shallow water of ten to 20 feet or so, but the time and effort of construction matched with immobility usually make other methods more appealing to the average wreck diver. If, however, you are doing a large excavation on a shallow site, a prop wash can be built by constructing a large tube with a 90 degree elbow. This tube has to be firmly mounted to the dive boat to capture her prop wash

Carl Fismer's boat with a Prop Wash securely mounted to the stern. Photo courtesy Carl Fismer.

and divert the force downward. The boat is usually anchored or moored at four points to assure location integrity. The two stern anchors take the most strain. When the engine is put into forward, the bottom is dusted away. According to treasure hunter, Carl Fismer, a safety cage can be mounted to the Prop Wash to allow divers to work while the unit is being used. Divers should stay clear of the boat when a Mail Box is in operation. According to THE UNDERWATER DIG by Robert Marx, a simple but ingenious signal system was achieved by using a weighted line attached to a horn on the boat. Divers could then quickly signal the surface to turn off or start up the Mail Box.

ARTIFACT RECOVERY

Finding an artifact is only half of the fun. Actually getting heavy objects off the bottom of the sea bed and onto the boat safely can be an even greater challenge. Many times I've heard divers say they located a beautiful china bowl but couldn't get to it, found a porthole, but it was still attached, or found a ceiling light, but it was still bolted on. To these divers this was the end of the story, but, in my eyes, these were only challenges to be met by careful planning, the proper tools and, of course, knowing the limitations of

Diver Steve Jonassen uses a davit to hoist a heavy porthole aboard the dive boat Wreck Valley. Photo by Daniel Berg.

63

individual experience. The ceiling light was easily wedged off with a chisel and a four pound sledge hammer. Remember all work done while using SCUBA must be controlled, so always stay calm. If you start to breathe heavily, STOP! You can always come back another day. The porthole swing plate I mentioned was retrieved after making a special push pin to tap out its hinge pin. The china bowl was a little more tricky, and my first two attempts failed. The steel plate which had the bowl covered would not budge even with a crow bar. It finally did with the help of a car scissor jack purchased at the local junk yard. Divers have also worked successfully with hacksaws and wedges. I recommend looking at each stubborn artifact as a challenge. Be persistent, but do not do anything that might endanger or push yourself beyond your limits.

Once a heavy artifact is free from the bottom, it must be brought to the surface. Use a lift bag for anything over 15 pounds. If someone is on the boat and knows that a bag is coming up, you can slowly add air until the object just begins to rise off the bottom. Be sure that none of your hoses or gear is caught on the bag. Then grab the artifact and lift it; the air in the lift bag will expand and slowly start to ascend. When using a lift bag, keep the bag in front of you, and keep your back into the current. This keeps the bag and the heavy artifact away from you as it rises. Believe me, you don't want to be underneath the bag. It only takes one bad knot, a leaky bag, or a big wave and the prized artifact could come crashing back down onto the wreck. As a side note, I usually attach an up line to my lift bag before sending it to the surface. The line is then attached to the wreck after the bag has surfaced. The main advantage is that the line will hold the bag close to the boat, and the current wont carry it away. The second reason is that if for any reason the lift bag does not stay on the surface, I can go back down on my next dive and follow the line to relocate the artifact. You can use a tether line reel, Jersey Reel or Line Ball as an up line. Once the artifact is on the surface, your last task is to get it onto the boat. Depending on the size and weight of your find and the size of the boat, this could be easy or very difficult. The best method is with some type of winch or block and tackle system. Remember diver safety comes first. Never let a diver get under or behind a heavy object as it is being pulled or winched on board. A mishap could be disastrous. As a side note, it's always a good idea to look at a large object while it is still there on the bottom and ask the question, will this fit on the boat? I know this sounds pretty silly, but I'm saying it only due to my own experience. In 1985, I ran my boat out to the wreck of the *Sandy Hook*. The *Sandy Hook* was a pilot boat that was sunk due to a collision with the Norwegian vessel, *Oslofjord*. Rick Schwarz, Dennis Berg and I descended and within ten minutes, I had sent a porthole to the surface. Unfortunately, it was still attached to a steel hull plate and required a 500 pound lift bag. Although we tried, we just couldn't get the cumbersome artifact onto the boat and had to cut it free.

ARTIFACT PRESERVATION

Preservation of artifacts is extremely important and requires not only time but often a little elbow grease as well. The process usually starts on the boat immediately after an artifact is found. The first and cardinal rule is to keep the artifact wet and not exposed to air until the preservation process can begin. This is extremely important with steel artifacts which start to rust immediately upon contact with air. Soaking in fresh water is best, but salt water will do fine temporarily. Even wrapping the item in plastic will usually keep in enough moisture until preservation can begin. I have listed below some cleaning and preservation methods for different materials. Some of these methods are non scientific and have been learned through my own as well as others experiences. Please use the information below at your own discretion.

BRASS and BRONZE

Both brass and bronze hold up very well in salt water. Although no preservation is needed, most brass or bronze artifacts usually need to be cleaned to some degree. Any encrustation can often be chipped off with wooden picks. Wood is used so the surface won't get scratched or marred.

Carl Fismer displays brass cannon balls recovered from a wreck sunk in 1631. Photo courtesy Carl Fismer.

Diver Keith Wipprecht and the telegraph he recovered from the tanker *Coimbra*, sunk on January 15, 1942. Photo courtesy Keith Wipprecht.

The first step is to soak the artifact in fresh water for about one month. This will usually leach out any chlorides and prevent the object from later turning green. To actually clean the object, several methods can be used. The first is to sand blast it or use glass beads to leave a clean dull finish. Then use a fine brass wire wheel on an electric drill or bench motor to polish.

Another method used to clean brass and bronze is electrolysis. An electrolysis bath is set up by immersing the artifact in an electrolyte solution, usually a 5% to 10% solution of caustic soda also known as sodium hydroxide or lye, and water and passing an electrical charge through the artifact. Rubber gloves, safety glasses and a rubberized apron should always be used when working with lye. To set up an electrolysis tank, start with a plastic container of a suitable size so that the artifact may be completely submerged, a car battery charger and an anode of stainless steel which has been attached to the positive side of a DC power source. Now connect the negative wire to the artifact and place it in the still empty tank. The anode should not be in contact with the artifact. The electrical current should be on before immersion of the artifact. It does not take much electricity to clean a brass artifact. For example, three amps is more than sufficient to clean a porthole. Of course, the voltage must be sufficient to achieve proper flow. The time period depends on the size, shape, and electrical current, but since this is cleaning and not preservation, it should not take more than a day.

Brad Sheard (left) and Dennis Kessler hold brass plaques recovered from the *Andrea Doria*. Photo courtesy Brad Sheard.

The author holds two rectangular brass portholes he recovered from the wreck of a World War II sub chaser. Photo by Steve Jonassen.

Finally, an acid bath can be used. Use a 50/50 solution of muriatic acid and water. Let the artifact soak, fully submerged, for a couple of days or until the artifact is clean. You will need to soak the brass or bronze in fresh water for a full month, changing the water every few days to leach out all of the acid. This soaking insures that your artifact will not turn green. A final polishing with a fine brass wire wheel or even by hand with a brillo pad will make the brass shine. As a final stage to any of the above listed methods, I suggest coating the polished brass with a clear poly-urethane spray, which helps to prevent the shine from dulling.

CERAMICS

Pottery, porcelain and china are all included in this category. The first rule is to immediately soak any item found in salt water in fresh water. Soak the item for approximately eight weeks, changing the water every day or so. I prefer to use warm water rinses followed by cold water baths during every change of water. The idea is to leach out as much salt as possible from the artifact. Steve Bielenda uses the toilet bowl tank as his artifact bath. His idea is logical because items placed in the tank are constantly being rinsed with fresh water each time the toilet is flushed. Hank Garvin recommends soaking china artifacts in a lemon juice bath. The mild acid in the lemon juice helps to leach out salt and should not harm any ornamental gold leaf on the china.

Carl Fismer holds a piece of pottery found on a Spanish treasure wreck sunk in Florida in 1715. Photo by Steve Frink, Courtesy Carl Fismer.

China recovered from the wreck of the Cunard liner *Oregon* (left) and the *Andrea Doria*. Courtesy Steve Bielenda collection. Photos by Daniel Berg.

After the initial soaking, use a warm water rinse with a mild soap solution. If calcium deposits are present, use a vinegar bath, but be careful; some decorative patterns, especially gold leaf, are very delicate. Soak in fresh water after the vinegar or lemon bath.

After the final rinsing, if the artifact still has its original glaze, this is all the preservation that is needed. If the object is porous, it is advisable to coat it with an acrylic plastic.

GLASS

Fortunately glass holds up fairly well underwater, even after decades of submersion. Usually bottles dating from the early 1800's to the present, found on or near shipwrecks, are in good condition. There are, of course, exceptions to every rule, and I have read reports of glass dating to the early 1700's that would crack after drying out. When intact bottles are found buried in silt or sand, they can be as clear as the day they were lost. However, if the wreck is in a strong current area or in a location where a lot of surge is present, the bottles can be dulled by the sand blasting effect of constantly tumbling around.

Bottles deep inside the World War I wreck of the *USS San Diego*. Photo by Jon Hulburt.

Diver Hank Garvin with bottles recovered from the *USS San Diego*. Photo by Steve Bielenda.

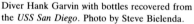

The authors collection of bottles recovered from a variety of shipwrecks. Photo by Daniel Berg.

In order to clean glass, all that is needed is fresh water, some powdered dish washing detergent and a little elbow grease. If stubborn stains are present, a 50% solution of muriatic acid and water can be used. Remember to wear plastic gloves and to rinse the artifact with fresh water after using acid. For bottles that are stained on the inside, use a bottle brush with a mud-like solution of detergent and water. If you don't have a bottle brush, just shake the sloppy mixture around. It will have enough abrasiveness to remove most stains without damaging the glass.

GOLD

Gold is amazing, and, depending on the quality, it is usually found as clean and shiny as new. Aaron Hirsh, a friend of mine, told me that the best method to preserve gold after recovery is to put it in a safe. Actually, he is right; very little is necessary to preserve this precious metal, and usually cleaning is all that is required. Sometimes gold may be found tarnished. Soaking in a 10% solution of nitric acid and water will usually remove any tarnish. I have found 10 karat gold that looked almost gray and very much like dull silver, but after a little polishing with a dremel held cotton buffing

Mike McMeekin uses a chemical kit to test a variety of gold artifacts. Photo by Daniel Berg.

Teddy Tucker found this magnificent emerald studded cross on the wreck of the 350 ton Spanish nao *San Pedro*, Bermuda. Photo courtesy Edna and Teddy Tucker.

Jack Haskins recovered this unique and priceless artifact from the *Capitiana* sunk in 1733, Florida. Photo courtesy Carl Fismer.

wheel, jewelers ruse, and some metal polish the gold gleamed. Gold can also be tested fairly easily and accurately with a karat testing chemical kit. This comes in real handy when trying to have an item appraised. The kit comes with a fine stone and a chemical solution for each karat rating. Simply rub a small amount of gold onto the stone and start out by dropping a drop of the mildest acid on to it. If it doesn't dissolve, go to the next stronger chemical and continue until the small scratch of gold dissolves. Each bottle is marked, so whichever was strong enough to dissolve the gold residue on the stone is the karat rating of the gold.

LEAD and TIN

Objects of lead and tin usually survive quite well while underwater. No preservation is usually needed, but any deposits of calcium or rust crustation can be removed by hand or with a pick. The white coating is usually lead oxide. This can be removed with a 10% solution of acetic acid or white vinegar. Be careful when soaking in acid or vinegar, if left for extended periods of time, damage will occur. After an acid bath, soak in warm water followed by cool water. Repeat the fresh water baths a few times to help remove any remaining acid. After immersion in a rubbing alcohol bath, allow to dry, then coat with clear plastic spray or coat with paraffin wax.

Diver Rick Schwarz recovered this lead sounding weight from the wreck of the *R.C. Mohawk*, New York. Photo by Daniel Berg.

Mike Burke found these lead crucifixes on the *Constellation* wreck, Bermuda. Photo by Daniel Berg.

Leather shoe recovered from the *San Diego* wreck.
Note the name carved into it's sole. Photo
courtesy Steve Bielenda.

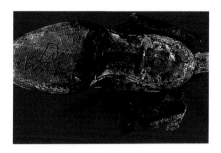

LEATHER

As with all organic material, leather should be soaked in fresh water for at
least two weeks; then it can be carefully brushed clean with a soft nylon
brush. The next step is to soak the artifact for two hours in a 50% solution of
alcohol and fresh water. Next use a 100% alcohol bath. After the object is
completely cleaned soak it in polyethylene glycol for approximately one
month.

SILVER

Silver holds up fairly well underwater, but most items such as coins will be
covered in a heavy black rust like coating. In fact, to the untrained eye,
silver coins usually look like junk until they are restored. First, remove as
much of the silver sulfide coating as possible; this can usually be picked off.
Depending on the item you can use a vinegar bath, electrolysis, or a
chemical bath followed by a cleaning with tooth paste and polishing with
silver polish. A dremel grinder with a fine wire wheel may even be used on

From left to right, Treasure hunters Jim Inman,
Carl Fismer and Todd Inman with silver coins
recovered from a Florida treasure wreck.
Courtesy Carl Fismer, Photo by Steve Frink.

some objects, then a cotton wheel and a fine jeweler's ruse compound. Be careful if you choose the dremel grinder, as the wire wheel will scratch into the artifact's surface. Charles Garrett offers a simple electrolysis method for cleaning coins in his book, TREASURE RECOVERY FROM SAND & SEA. His method uses an electrolyte solution of one teaspoon of citric acid and a half teaspoon of salt dissolved in one cup of water. The positive side of a three to six volt power supply is attached to a stainless steel anode on one side of the glass, and an alligator clip is used to attach the negative side to the coin which is placed on the other side of the glass. The current that flows through the solution will loosen any encrustation.

STEEL and IRON

Steel and iron are the most difficult to preserve. Severe corrosion is usually the problem. The first step is to remove any loose rust or encrustation. This can be done by scraping, sandblasting or tapping lightly with a hammer. After the object is cleaned, the metal has to be preserved. Electrochemical or an electrolysis bath can be used, or, if the item is too large to be submerged in a bath, the diver can simply heavily paint the artifact to seal the object from the elements. This method does not prevent corrosion from within but is used frequently on large anchors which would be hard to soak. For an electrochemical bath, smaller items can be soaked in a 10% solution of sodium hydroxide and 90% water. Note that the solution should be kept in a sealed plastic container, and plastic gloves should always be used. Soak the item for two to six months, depending on its size. Some then choose to dry the artifact completely and coat it with polyurethene or paint. Drying of small artifacts can be done in an oven, 200 degrees for 12-24 hours. Larger items can be heated with a torch. Another sealing method would be to place

Steel fluted anchor raised by Steve Jonassen (left) and Dan Berg, from the *USS Tarantula*. Photo by Bill Campbell.

Steve Jonassen starts the preservation process by sandblasting away rust and encrustation. Photo by Daniel Berg.

it in a bath of the same solution and surround the object with zinc plates or zinc chips. The solution will bubble for about two weeks. When the artifact is removed and rinsed off, it will have a white coating which can be left on or removed with a 5% solution of sulfuric acid. The next step is to soak it in running fresh water for approximately two days. Dry the item completely and coat the exterior with polyurethene, paraffin wax or paint. The exterior coating seals the iron from contact with air and moisture and prevents future corrosion.

An electrolysis bath can be set up as described in the brass and bronze section of this book. Remember that the electrolysis used for brass is for cleaning and when used on steel is for preservation. The duration will vary from several days to several weeks depending on the size and age of the object. According to THE UNDERWATER DIG by Robert Marx, the current, "should be five amperes for every 25 square inches of the objects surface". The artifact should be removed from the bath while the power is still on. The artifact should then be emersed in a fresh water bath and brushed clean. The water should be changed regularly for about two weeks. Drying and sealing is identical to the electrochemical method listed above.

UNGLAZED POTTERY

Unglazed Pottery is more porous than china or glass and when found in salt water, you have to realize that this pottery allows more salt to saturate it than glazed china does. Once brought up from depth, the salt inside an artifact that is not preserved correctly will dry, crystalize and cause cracking and possible destruction to the artifact.

The first rule is to prevent the artifact from drying out. The best immediate choice is a fresh water bath, but if you're on a boat and fresh water is not available, salt water will due. For the car ride home, wrap the objects in

Unglazed Pottery is more porous than china. Most artifacts require immediate preservation. Photo by Carl Fismer.

plastic to keep in any moisture and prevent crystallization. Again as with ceramics, the first step to preservation is to leach out as much salt and chlorides as possible. For small objects, the holding tank of a toilet bowl works fine; otherwise, soak in fresh water for approximately eight weeks, changing the water every couple of days. The next step is to soak the item in a bath of rubbing alcohol for three to four hours. Afterwards, let the artifact dry completely, which may take a few days. Drying can be assisted with an alcohol bath. Then it is advised to coat the artifact with a clear polyurethane spray or as Carl Fismer, a noted treasure hunter, recommends paint with a mixture of Elmers glue and water.

WOOD

Wood is difficult and time consuming to preserve. However, artifacts like rifle stocks, cargo crates with ink writing and dead eyes tempt the novice and even the experienced wreck diver to try. The problem is that when a wood item that has been submerged for years or even decades is dried out, it will shrink and crack. According to THE UNDERWATER DIG by Robert Marx, "When waterlogged wood is allowed to dry out, the evaporation of water from its degenerated inner cellulose and cells will cause the remaining outer cell walls to collapse from surface tension". We have to preserve each wood artifact by removing all water and salt from the inner cell structure while strengthening the wood's cell structure.

Diver Steve Jonassen holds a wood crate recovered from the wreck of the freight steamer *Iberia*, New York. Photo by Daniel Berg.

The author Daniel Berg recovered this wood dead eye from the *Steel Mast Wreck* in Florida. Photo by Dennis Berg.

Start off by keeping the object immersed in fresh water. Alternate warm and cool water. This rinse stage can go on for weeks or months, depending on the size, thickness and particular type of wood. The best scientific preservation method is impregnation with a 60% solution of polyethylene glycol also known as PEG or carbo wax. Polyethylene glycol penetrates into the cell structure of the wood. In basic terms, it keeps each cell from shrinking and, therefore, greatly reduces any overall cracking. Artifacts should be submerged for a sufficient period of time that allows full penetration. For example, a wood dead eye may take six months, a wood rib one to two years. Polyethylene glycol can be purchased at chemists shops, but it is costly.

Another method, which is not scientific by any means, may be used at the reader's discretion. After the rinse stage which should last from two to 12 months depending on thickness, completely dry the object by using an alcohol bath. Next, coat it heavily with clear polyurethane. The artifact will shrink and crack but hopefully not too badly. The polyurethene coating will also protect any ink writing on the artifact.

ARTIFACT PRESENTATION

Recreational divers have two distinct views on what should be done to present an artifact for display. On one side, some divers clean and polish every brass piece they recover. On the other side, some divers preserve but don't clean their objects at all, allowing whatever rust, barnacles or coral to vividly show to all the origin of the artifact.

I've found that each artifact has to be looked at individually. Some need cleaning to show the original beauty, while others need to be preserved then left alone. Most need certain key areas to be polished while leaving barnacles and some growth in place to give immediate identification that the artifact has been found in the sea. As an example of this, I recently was diving on a World War I Navy vessel with some friends. When we all retrieved some brass valves and brought them home, most were completely covered in a conglomeration of rust from the steel the valves were lying on. Two weeks later, we compared our valves. Some were left covered in rust, which truthfully looked like a hunk of junk rather than a brass artifact. Some were polished to a high gloss which must have taken considerable time and effort and only resulted in looking like a piece of brass purchased in the local hardware store. I had left one of my valves covered in rust then chiseled away the rust that covered the wheel. I then cleaned and polished the wheel while leaving the rest covered or fossilized. We all agreed that this was the best of both worlds. This method can be adapted to almost any artifact. Say

This standing lamp was made from a gun powder canister the author recovered from the *USS San Diego*. Photo by Steve Jonassen.

The author made this clock from a small brass porthole. Photo by Daniel Berg

A series of small portholes have been mounted as lights in the authors attic office. Photo by Daniel Berg.

This brass door frame, which was recovered from the *USS San Diego* by the author and Bill Campbell, was converted into a coffee table. Photo by Daniel Berg.

for example, that you had recovered a porthole and had already cleaned and polished the item. Simply find a few barnacles and glue them to the artifact in a couple of places; you'll be amazed at how much more authentic and historic your treasure will look.

Artifact presentation goes far beyond deciding how to clean an item. Many items can be put back into use. I have a ship's brass door frame mounted as an entrance into my office, a porthole as a window, another brass frame made into a coffee table, a standing lamp made from a gunpowder canister and brass valve wheels mounted onto my garden hose faucets. Although this is a bit extreme, it's not uncommon for divers to use recovered china or silverware or to electrify a cage lamp and hang it on the wall. Small portholes can easily be made into clocks or they make beautiful picture frames. Some artifacts can be mounted and hung from the wall, while some should simply sit on a shelf. Still others can be used and enjoyed every day.

SHIPWRECK PHOTOGRAPHY

By Jozef Koppelman

Taking photographs underwater has fascinated divers for years. With a little luck and a lot of skill, a diver can bring home the beauty of the undersea world for all to enjoy. Wreck photography is just a little more demanding than but a lot more rewarding than fish or reef photos. Picture a diver cruising down a darkened corridor, with only small rays of ambient light penetrating through corroded holes in the ceiling above him. On the silt covered floor, he finds a china dish with a lobster sitting next to it. He snaps three pictures before catching the lobster and picking up the dish. These photographs will be outstanding, that is if they come out. A problem involved in photography in and around shipwrecks is that the diver must be able to operate all of his wreck diving equipment and camera gear while not kicking up any sediment. He also has to contend with the darkness inside a wreck.

One recommendation is that you do not start photographing too early in your dive career. You should be able to hover effortlessly and check your air, time, depth and anchor location as second nature first. If you are new to wreck diving, you should also enjoy a period of exploration and familiarization. Once you commit to the task of making underwater images, you are really taking on an underwater job, but the satisfaction of producing a fine picture quickly diminishes the memory of all the challenges that preceded its making. This includes dollars spent, equipment failure, bad visibility, throwaway rolls and the one great shot that got away. Before diving into a wreck with a camera in hand, streamline yourself even more

Shipwreck Photography

The author deep inside the Coast Guard cutter Duane, Florida. Photo by Jozef Koppelman.

Chris Villanti free dives the *Plane Wreck* in Cozumel. Photo by Jozef Koppelman.

Photographer Joe Koppelman prepares to dive the *Windjammer* wreck, Bonaire. Photo by Frank Valenti.

Frank Valenti explores the stern of the *Proteus* in North Carolina. Photo by Jozef Koppelman.

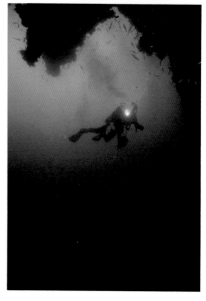

Divers descend to the *R.P. Resor* off Long Island, New York. Photo by Jozef Koppelman.

Mark Silverstein on the *Andrea Doria's* promenade deck. Photo by Jozef Koppelman.

Bow of the *Windjammer* wreck, Bonaire. Photo by Jozef Koppelman.

Diver and live mines on the deck of the *San Francisco Maru*, Truk Lagoon. Photo by Jozef Koppelman.

The Author on the wreck of the Coast Guard cutter Duane, Florida. Photo by Jozef Koppelman."

than normal. You may want to leave your tools and bug bag on the boat since it's hard to do it all. In regard to air supply for deep wrecks, many feel the twin tank independent regulator rig is the ultimate in safety. Photographers, however, often opt for doubles with a single regulator and pony. Given the complexity of underwater photography, this set up eliminates the need to switch air sources while underwater.

Assuming that those wishing to photograph shipwrecks will find proper instruction for basic underwater photography, we will then start with some standard equipment and techniques. Camera systems vary in design, function and price. One of the most popular used today is the Nikonos body. For most photography on shipwrecks, the diver will choose a wide angle lense, either a 15mm or the more economical 20mm. This is not saying that macro photos are never taken on shipwrecks. Many worthwhile subjects are found living on wrecks, but, for the most part, taking macro photographs on a reef is exactly the same as taking macro photos on a wreck. We want wide angle lenses, so we can capture as much wreckage as possible while being as close to the subject as possible. A powerful, wide angle strobe is also essential. One with a modeling light is also very useful. Wreck photography is usually a battle against the lack of light. To deal with the darkness inside a wreck and to avoid fumbling around with a light in one hand and a camera in the other, many serious photographers mount a dive light to their camera system. Others wear a head or helmet mounted dive light or mount a small modeling light onto the strobe. Dealing with the always present silt and sediment inside shipwrecks can be solved with speed. The wreck photographer doesn't have the luxury of spending five minutes setting up for the shot or making a camera adjustment to bracket each shot. He has to shoot the picture before any silt gets disturbed. If he is too slow, the suspended particles will ruin his photo opportunity. Since time is of the essence, wreck divers have learned to bracket their photographs by taking a series of shoots as they approach a subject. This is done without changing any camera or strobe settings. Another method is to have the strobe hand held off the camera. This lets the photographer bracket the exposure by moving the strobe closer or further from the subject while positioning the strobe to reduce back scatter, the incidental illumination of suspended particles in the water.

Film must be tailored to your purposes and to the anticipated conditions. For casual viewing, color negative, print film is very exposure tolerant. If, however, you pursue photography seriously, transparency slide film shoud by your preference, especially if you hope to have your work published. Tropical sunny weather and shallow water allow for a medium speed film. Kodachrome, Fuji or Ectkachrome 100 will do fine. The latter two films employ E-6 processing which allows for quick processing and is even available on many live aboard dive boats. E-6 processing also allows for pushing or increasing of film speed in processing, at a small sacrifice to grain and contrast. On deeper wrecks or in less than ideal conditions, faster films like K200, E400 or Fugi 400 can be employed. Even with recent technological improvements, ultra fast films are more grainy and are more effective in depicting atmospheric shots. The photographer should take light readings and then set the aperture accordingly.

Using a model will add visual interest to many wreck photographs. The model can be used in two ways: as a secondary element for scale and to add visual interest. Secondly, the diver can be brought closer to become the more dominant feature in the image. Try not to have the model over-pose but instead rely on their curiosity in exploring the wreck. One trick is to have your model use a light. It adds immeasurably to the interest and can also highlight a particular object. Another recommended technique is to shoot when the model is exhaling. The finished image will be much more dynamic if bubbles are shown rising to the surface.

You will note the absence of any composition guidelines. This is because it is our belief that everyone has an individual vision. Once diving and photographic techniques have been honed, your own artistic view will be your most valuable asset in expressing your own visions of the sea.

Shipwrecks offer the underwater photographer an endless amount of photo opportunities. Whether you're photographing a porthole, fish, lobster or any of the other majestic photo opportunities shipwrecks offer, divers will almost certainly never run out of things to photograph.

LOBSTERING

Shipwrecks have been related to being an oasis in the middle of a barren desert of sand. It is true that fish and all types of marine life thrive in and around wrecks because the wreck becomes an artificial reef. Cold water lobsters or Maine lobsters (Homarus americanus) also make their home in and around northeast shipwrecks. In fact, cold water lobsters are the main attraction of some shipwrecks. Before catching a lobster make sure to check out all local laws. Many states have minimum or maximum size regulations and require divers to have a lobster permit.

Lobsters are known to divers as bugs and they are delicious, once captured and cooked that is. To catch a lobster, the diver must first find it. Usually the diver will swim around, looking into every hole with his light until he sees the claws or antenna. The lobster has a great defense with its claws; in fact, larger bugs are said to be able to crush a coke bottle. As a rule, larger lobsters are slower than their younger counterparts. In any case, no matter what the size of the creature, getting bit can be quite painful. The diver must position himself to make what may be his only attempt at catching his prey. The diver must then quickly thrust his hand into the hole, grabbing the lobster just behind or on top of its claws. If the lobster is deep into the hole, you can pin its claws down while slowly working your fingers up its body into position. When the lobster is caught, simply pull it out and put it tail first into a catch bag. Lobsters swim backwards, so, by inserting them tail first, we make sure they swim into and not out of the bag. This, of course, was an overly simplified scenario. The art of lobstering goes far beyond. For example, the true bug fanatic knows which shipwrecks hold more lobsters, usually low lying wood wrecks which aren't visited that often. They also know tricks to get the big bugs out of their deep holes. For example, when a lobster is deep into a pipe and can't be reached from either end, the diver can try to beat the pipe with a sledge hammer. The lobster will usually try to escape the noise and can then be tracked down and caught. When a big bug is deep in a blind hole, you can try a few tricks: first try catching a smaller lobster and releasing it into the bigger bug's hole. Usually the larger bug will quickly come out to guard its territory against the intruder. When it comes close to the opening, grab it. Another trick is to bait the lobster by putting a

A lobster has a great defense with its claws.
Photo by Bill Campbell.

Dan Berg Holds a lobster caught off Long Island. Photo by Rick Schwarz.

A diver must quickly thrust his hand into the hole, grabbing the lobster just behind it's claws. Here diver Ed Tiedemann has captured a good size lobster. Photo by Jeanne Tiedemann.

small piece of fish or mussel meat at the entrance to its hole. After a few minutes, it may decide to come out for dinner. The best trick I know for consistently catching lobsters is to know where the best holes are on a wreck. Lobsters are very territorial and seem to live in a hierarchy of sorts. The biggest lobster gets the best hole to call home. Once you have found one big lobster, make a mental note of where it was caught and simply return on consecutive dives. You will most likely find another large lobster living in the same hole. Some divers use tickle sticks made from either collapsible car antennas or wrapped up wire that can be unwrapped and bent into almost any shape in order to get it in behind the bug. They then touch the bug's tail, and the lobster walks right into their hands. Another trick is to tape a lobster size gauge onto a dive light. This way very little time is wasted. You find, catch and check the bug's size without having to fumble around, putting your light down or trying to find the gauge. A lobster size gauge measures the length of its carapace. That is the distance from the eye socket to the beginning of the tail. Remember to always check the lobster's underside. If it has eggs on the underside of its tail, release it back into its hole to assure a good supply for future years. As with most things, the more you practice, the better you will become, not only in finding and catching lobsters, but also in putting smiles on the faces of your family back home who will surely enjoy eating your catch.

SPEAR FISHING

Ron Molaro on the *R.P. Resor*

The author holds a ten pound black fish taken in an area known as Wreck Valley. Photo by Bill Campbell.

Divers Bill Campbell (left) and Jay Lipari with a days catch. Photo courtesy of Bill Campbell.

Photo by Jozef Koppelman.

Spear Fishing

Spear fishing is an art all in itself. This exciting sport is enhanced through shipwrecks because wrecks attract such a wealth of aquatic life. Spear fishing on a shipwreck is an exciting change from open water diving or spearing under bridges. Although I make no claim to be a world class spear fisherman, I have always found it quite easy to bring home dinner while exploring the sunken remains of ships. In the New York, New Jersey area, black fish are the prized catch. These tasty fish with pure white meat are very difficult to catch on hook and line. Fishermen are more than happy catching fish in the two to four pound class, but divers are a little more spoiled. In fact, its been about four years since I've taken a fish under five pounds. The normal catch is one big fish of ten to 12 pounds. We leave the little ones to grow up and eat the bait of local fishermen. In 1988, Bill Campbell dove the wreck of the *Yankee*, a coastwise steamer sunk in 1919, and brought up an 18 pound black fish. Although this is not quite a record fish, it is the largest specimen of this species I have ever seen and is certainly impressive, especially after hearing the story behind its capture. First of all, Bill didn't even have a spear gun; he was just looking around for lobsters when he found the huge fish amongst some wreckage. Bill took out his dive knife and stabbed the fish, trying to hold it against the sand bottom so it couldn't escape. The fish was so strong that it yanked the knife right out of Bill's hands, and swam away with the knife still in its side. Bill swam after the fish and soon found his knife sitting in the sand. He was amazed that he could actually see a blood trail floating just off the bottom. After imitating a blood hound for a few minutes, he relocated his prized fish wedged between two steel hull plates. A photograph of Bill and his fish appeared in the next issue of the LONG ISLAND FISHERMAN Magazine.

In other areas of the world, divers tell similar stories. Of course, the type of fish is different but the excitement and rewards of spear fishing on shipwrecks are always the same.

A few basic rules to follow are never spear in limited visibility when other divers are in the area. The line on a gun should be no longer than one half the visibility. Caribbean divers who are used to 100 feet or more in visibility may laugh at this rule, but let them experience four feet of visibility with the knowledge that somebody is spear fishing with six feet of line. It's quite uncomfortable. Move very slowly so as not to spook your prey, or stay motionless and let the fish come to you. A good friend of mine, Jim D'Alessio, was always very good at this. I used to watch him sit inside a tug boat wreck with his spear aimed out a porthole. When a big fish came by, Jim shot it, pulled it in and reloaded. My rule is never to take more fish than you're going to eat.

SUGGESTED READING

Other Books by the Author

Berg, Daniel and Denise
  Bermuda Shipwrecks
  Aqua Explorers, Inc. (1991)

Berg, Daniel and Denise
  Florida Shipwrecks
  Aqua Explorers, Inc. (1991)

Berg, Daniel
  Shore Diver
  Aqua Explorers, Inc. (1987)

Berg, Daniel
  Wreck Valley
  Aqua Explorers, Inc. (1986)

Berg, Daniel
  Wreck Valley Vol II
  Aqua Explorers, Inc. (1990)

Berg, Daniel and Denise
  Tropical Shipwrecks
  Aqua Explorers, Inc. (1989)

Wreck Diving Books

Gentile, Gary
  Advanced Wreck Diving Guide
  Cornell Maritime Press. (1988)

INDEX

8/12

Send For Our
FREE
Catalog of Dive Publications
Aqua Explorers, Inc.
Po Box 116
East Rockaway, NY 11518
Phone/Fax (516) 868-2658